FUTURE STOCKS

Also by Robert Metz

How to Shake the Money Tree

The Tax-Conscious Investor

Franchising: How to Select a Business of Your Own

CBS: Reflections in a Bloodshot Eye

Jackpot! Everything You Need to Know About Smart Money Investing in the New Wall Street

The Today Show

The Tonight Show

FUTURE STOCKS

INVESTING FOR PROFIT IN THE GROWTH
STOCKS OF THE 1980S

Robert Metz

82-4677

HARPER & ROW, PUBLISHERS, New York

Cambridge, Philadelphia, San Francisco
London, Mexico City, São Paulo, Sydney

1817

THE OZARKS REGIONAL LIBRARY
217 EAST DICKSON STREET
FAYETTEVILLE, ARK. 72701

To Elizabeth with love and Seashells

This book offers only general investment observations based on the author's experience and makes no specific recommendations.

It is intended and written to provide the author's opinions in regard to the subject matter covered. The author and the publisher are not engaged in rendering legal, accounting or other professional advice and the reader should seek the services of a qualified professional for such advice.

The author and the publisher cannot be held responsible for any loss incurred as a result of the application of any of the information in this publication.

FUTURE STOCKS. Copyright © 1982 by Robert Metz. All rights reserved. Printed in the United States of America. No part of this book may be used or reproduced in any manner whatsoever without written permission except in the case of brief quotations embodied in critical articles and reviews. For information address Harper & Row. Publishers, Inc., 10 East 53rd Street, New York, N.Y. 10022. Published simultaneously in Canada by Fitzhenry & Whiteside Limited, Toronto.

FIRST EDITION

Designer: Sidney Feinberg

Library of Congress Cataloging in Publication Data

Metz, Robert.
  Future stocks.
  Includes index.
  1. Stocks. 2. Investments. I. Title. II. Title:
Growth stocks of the 1980's.
HG4661.M45 1982   332.63'22   81-47667
ISBN 0-06-014945-0   AACR2

82 83 84 85 86 10 9 8 7 6 5 4 3 2 1

Contents

Acknowledgments   xi

Introduction   1

   A Once-in-a-Lifetime Opportunity, 1
   The Importance of the New Era Cannot Be Overstated, 2
   Nailing Down Profits, 3
   Picking and Choosing for Big Rewards, 3
   Yesterplays, 4
   Mining Wall Street's Gold, 5
   What's a Computer? 6
   Your Rosetta Stone to Riches, 6
   Golden Oldies That Paid Off, 7

Part I
Entering the World of High Technology

1. The New High-Technology Revolution and Low-Cost Energy   11

   Enter the Fabulous Chip, 12
   The Great Leap Forward, 12
   Sifting Sand, 13
   Giant Steps into the Future, 14
   Eniac to the Rescue? 15
   Microprocessor Razzle-Dazzle, 16
   The New Age of Electronics Arrives, 17
   The Microcomputer as Superclerk, 18

Sun Power Does It Best, 19
The Ever-Present Microprocessor, 19
Self-Sufficiency in Fuel: Will It Ever Happen Again? 19
Photovoltaics: The Second Miracle of Silicon, 20
The Semiconductor as the "New Crude," 20
Whither Growth? 21
The Era of Future Stocks, 22
Sharing the Wealth, 22
New Markets for Old Companies, 23
The Highly Rewarding Quest for Values, 24
Household Names Anyone? 25

2. What Is Growth? 27

The "T. Rowe" Way to Go, 27
"Avon Calling!" Recounting a Fabulous Stock Market Success Story, 29
The Quarter-Million-Dollar Bonanza Club, 31
Commodore: The Ultimate Winner, 31
Buffett on the Elusive Nature of Bargains, 34
What Then Are the Growth Stock Criteria? 35
The Magnificent Leveraging Effect of Debt on Future Stock Profits, 36
Contrariwise: Avoid Companies with Heavy Short-Term Debt, 36
The Investor's Back Door Entry to Low-Cost Future Stocks, 37
The Outsider's Inside Information, 38
Mainstream High-Tech Profit Generators, 39
Mutual Admiration Societies, 40

Part II
Zeroing in on Profits

Introduction: The Road to Riches, 43
Let the Author Be Your Proxy in the Executive Suite and in Wall Street's Inner Sanctum, 43
"Information, Please," 44
Discovering Those Winning Techniques, 45

3. Microprocessors: Nucleus of Change 47

The Classic Start-Up, 47
The Start-Up of Genentech, 47
The Ruinous Fad Stock Syndrome, 48
Intel: Little David Sidesteps the Giants, 49
Intel: Take Three, 49
The Hard-Nosed But Informal Atmosphere for Innovation, 50
Thriving Silicon Valley, 51
Start-Ups: Not Habit-Forming Perhaps, But Certainly Instructive, 52
The Luck of an Idea, 53

Contents

The Right Technology for an Exploding Market . . ., 54
. . . and Prices to Match, 54
On the Importance of Management, 56
Innovating for Profitable New Markets, 57
The "Exploding Market" Syndrome, 57
Innovation for the Future, 58
Why Debt May Be Essential, 59
What Might Have Been, 60
Ideology in High Technology, 60
Two Key Strategies for High-Tech Profits, 61
Jerry Sanders: The Dream Merchant, 61
An Important Ingredient for High-Tech Success: Environment, 62
Unsinkable by Doing the Unthinkable: Winning with Superior Product, 62
Up AMD and the Industry Too, 63
Rocketing to the Stars on Dream Power, 64
Doing It the Hard Way, 65
Superior Products Set the New Higher Standard: Bye-Bye Blackbird, 66
"Money Is the World's Report Card," 67

4. Minicomputers and the Office of the Future (Two High-Technology Turnarounds)   69

Electronic Overkill, 69
Explosive Growth in Mini-Power, 70
High-Tech Marketing Strategy: Sidestep IBM, 71
Digital Equipment Corporation: Junior IBM? 71
Try Soft Focus for a Clearer Picture, 72
The Office of the Future, 72
Wang: Diehard Original, 73
Exciting New Avenues to Profits for Minimakers, 73
An Wang: No Communist He, 74
The Turnaround, 75
Outguessing the Pros: Most Won't Notice Return on Equity Is Soaring 'Til You've Made Your Bundle, 75
The Smartest Computer Companies Hold the Customer's Hand, 77
Test of Excellence: Sleeping Giant Wakes, Smaller Rival Still Outruns Him, 78
Wang Has Scored Heavily with Borrowed Capital, 79
On the Importance of Being Loyal to High-Tech Companies, 80
Datapoint: Another Classic Turnaround, 81
The Drones and the Queen Bees, 82
Overlooked Opportunity, 85

5. Service for Supergrowth   86

The Old Piano Roll Blues, 86
Brute Force or Electronic Judo? 87
Survival of the Fittest, 89
May We Hear from a Pioneer, Please? 90

Let's Talk Automatic Data Processing, Inc., 91
Putting Payroll in Perspective, 91
The Better Mouse Trap May Be a Hard Sell, 92
An Important Aside, 93
Growing Up with ADP, 93
Enter Computers, Slowly, 94
To the Industry, Then, 96
Opening the Passages of the Corporate Memory, 96
Name, Rank, and Serial Number, Please, 97
Enter Data Base Management, 98
Cullinane Database Systems to the Rescue, 98
The Cullinane? 99
Shared Medical Systems Cures Hospital Ills, 100
The Network Approach, 101
From Smaller to Larger Hospitals? 102
What Multiple? 103

6. CAD/CAM Does It Best — 105

Scenario: Modern Times Revisited, 105
Look Ma, No Pencil! 106
Two-to-One Productivity Gains, 107
The Exploding Markets for CAD/CAM, 108
CAD/CAM Candidates, 109
Marketing Essential: Holding Share of Market, 109
Computervision Draws the Markets, 110
Big Dollars for R&D, 111
Some Contenders, 111
Faulty Perceptions on Wall Street, 113
Harris to the Rescue, 113
Cross & Trecker: Born-Again Growth Company, 114
No Ho-Hum Machine Tool Company, 114
Rolling with the Punch Press, 115
What's to Come, 115

7. Long Shots in Solar Power — 118

Solar Power Through High Technology: Will It Short-Circuit the Power Companies Soon, 118
Santa Claus on the Roof, 119
Texas Instruments: Born-Again Growth Stock? 120
Down the Pricing Curve, 120
Jack Kilby: Inventor, 121
Shine the Light over Here, Please, 122
Making the Connection, 123
Potent Beads of Power, 123
A Comforting Margin for Error, 124

Contents

Power to the People, 125
Better Late Than Never, 126
Future Stock Seekers: Watch for the Departure of Key Designers from Major Companies, 126
A Hybrid Approach to Financing That Can Serve Seekers of High-Tech Profits in Major Companies, 127
The Big Picture, 128

Part III
Investment Strategies: How to Buy and, Occasionally, How to Sell

8. When to Pay an Outrageous Multiple; What Tests to Employ 131

On the Origin of Top Management, 133
Tandem: The Computer That Never Breaks Down, 133
Tie Them Together and Hope, 134
Perpetual Motion Computers, 135
The Day the Computer Bombed Cleveland, 136
Tandem's Solution, 136
Tandem Leads the Way, 137
The Cray Advantage, 138
Mini-Markets for Supercomputers? 139
And Then There Was Rolm, 142
Tests: Fundamentals First, Then the Numbers Game, 145
Fundamentally Overvalued? 145
Tandy Is Dandy, 146
Different Strokes for Special Folks: Market Cap/Over Revenues, 147
The P/E Deflator: Putting Those Lofty P/Es in Perspective, 147
The Rowe Price 2:1 Ratio Rule: Testing Relative Value of Growth Stocks, 148
The Seldom-Traveled Avenue to Riches: High Returns and Value Added, 152
Prime-Time Investing, 153
Everyman's Bottom Line: Bounding Share Price Appreciation, 154
A $10,000 Investment in Prime in 1975 Was Worth $800,000 by 1981, 154
Winning Combo: High ROE Plus Rising Book, 155
Building for the Future: Those Critical First-Time Buyers, 157
The Other Side of the Coin: Why Repeat Business Is Important, 157

9. Some Additional Buy Strategies 159

When to Buy Them, 159
The Low-High Theory of Investment, 159
Back to the Drawing Board, 160
Fisher of Stocks, 161
Love Somebody—But Never Love a Stock, 162
Let George Do It, 163

10. Bailing Out: How Broad the Pond? How High the Moon? 165
   Padtime for Bonzo, 166
   Wringing the Market Dry, 167
   Premiums for Slow Growth, 168
   Disaster and Greed, Its Handmaiden, 168
   Question: When 15 Beats 100, 169
   Growth Ad Infinitum? 169
   World Champion Chicken Plucker, 170
   IBM: The Exceptional Case? 171
   IBM: New Directions, 172
   Break Up IBM!, 173
   The End of a Golden Era, 173

11. Stock Futures: 27 Potential Winners 176
    27 Stepping Stones to Success, 177

12. The New Beginning 189

Index 191

Acknowledgments

When I began this book, I knew little about the arcane world of computers apart from what I had learned in several years of working at a word processing computer terminal at *The New York Times*. But like any intelligent layman in an increasingly computerized world, I sensed the importance of the new thrust in high technology.

After delving into the subject I learned two things: Bright though I believed to be the future of high-technology stocks, I had enormously underestimated their prospects. This I learned from experts, analysts, contacts in the field, and executives who gave generously of their time and talents.

No list of sources will be complete, as even casual contacts provided vital information. The individuals listed below were particularly helpful and encouraging.

I start with the man who did the most: Donald W. Mitchell, of the Cambridge, Mass., consulting firm, Mitchell and Company. Don read the manuscript, helped correct it, and then offered scores of hints for investors that would help steer them into the most promising shares. He then gave the galleys a careful reading to make sure no errors had crept in during the editing process. His most recent venture, Mitchell Investment Management Company, Inc., was formed to select stocks like those discussed in this book.

George J. Stasen, of Medical Technology, Inc., Flourtown, Pa., was helpful from the beginning, when he confirmed my suspicions that something important was happening in the high-technology world. He has given his time selflessly.

Stephen McGruder, of Eberstadt Asset Management, made meticulous notes while reading the manuscript and helped correct a number of technical errors. So did Tom Kurlak, high-technology stock analyst for Merrill Lynch, Pierce, Fenner & Smith. John Westergaard, of the Equity Research Associates division of Ladenburg Thalman & Co., offered much time and assistance.

John was one of several who offered "stock futures" for Chapter 11. The others were Steve McGruder, Jim Magid and Faith Griffin of L. F. Rothschild, Unterberg Towbin, and Otis Bradley, of Alex Brown & Co. Alfred Berkeley, of that firm, was also most cooperative and helpful—particularly in explaining software concepts to me. Robert Benezre, of the same firm, supplied the information on Flow General.

(Several stock future notes were compiled by the author from various sources.)

I thank Ulric and Frederica Weil, of Morgan Stanley, who supplied research information on Tandem Computer, among other companies. John E. McGinty, of First Boston Corporation, helped with Cross & Trecker Corp.

Special thanks to John Sims, who saved me much embarrassment.

The Morgan Stanley & Co. *Electronics* newsletter written by Benjamin M. Rosen was a key source for the story of Texas Instruments' work with solar panels.

I know that I have left out many others, but trust those who helped will understand.

I accept full responsibility for any misplaced emphasis and for outright errors, though I trust that with the assistance of so many experts, I have kept errata to a minimum.

Introduction

> "I've been rich and I've been poor; rich is better."
> —SOPHIE TUCKER

A Once-in-a-Lifetime Opportunity

Not since the twenty years following World War II have investors had such a golden opportunity in the stock market as they have today. Now, as then, the market is onto high technology. Make no mistake about it, latter-day IBMs and Xeroxes will star.

The action will be swift and immensely profitable for those who seize the initiative.

Specifically, companies that are in the forefront of computer research and development will lead the way as the world whirls out of its centuries-old paper and ink orbit into an exciting new configuration—that of electronic bits on computer memory devices.

This is not a one-shot guess-the-right-stock-and-win proposition. A dozen producers of microprocessors, and scores of users of microprocessor end products—data and word processors, for example—will throw off such enormous profits that their shares will soar; manufacturers of specialized computers and word processors, companies with vast data banks, and makers of such mundane components as ceramic capacitors will all benefit. Hospital management companies, builders of body scanners, and bioengineers among the health care companies will participate, as will suppliers to the energy companies, telecommunications companies, and builders of solar cells. *Investors shrewd enough to spot the trends can experience tenfold profits in a decade*—or do even better in less time, as holders have done with their investments in such high-technology companies as Commodore International, American Medical International, Wang Computer, and Rolm Corporation.

The Importance of the New Era Cannot Be Overstated

Mainframe computers were the precursors of these remarkable computers on chips—and superbly managed IBM became the darling of the first wave, rewarding its owners handsomely.

But it was the invention of the thumbnail-sized microprocessor in 1970, the so-called computer on a chip by Intel, that set the stage for current advances—advances that are changing the way the world works in a fundamental manner. These bits of silicon are capable of feats of mathematical prowess and information processing so prodigious they would boggle the mind of a nineteenth-century savant. With the invention of the low-cost microprocessor, the era of enormously expensive computers is over.

But the microprocessor drama is only beginning. We are on the threshold of even more impressive electronic miracles. To wit: Intel has developed a micromainframe computer no bigger than a desk-top terminal itself that is as powerful as IBM's best large computers of the late 1970s. Though much slower than the IBM machines, the new device, announced in early 1981, will cost pennies by comparison and will tackle a variety of tasks so diverse and awe-inspiring that the inventors haven't begun to plumb its potential.

Meantime, the microprocessor has spawned entire new subindustries with equally exciting promise for investors. For example: Cray Research's scientific computers are currently the most powerful at work—capable of processing hundreds of thousands of calculations in a second though the superbly designed machines fit into boxes no bigger than filing cabinets. Cray anticipates that its next generation of machines will make possible highly accurate weather forecasts in minutes, a feat that took as long as 27 hours just a few years ago.

Introduction

Nailing Down Profits

A $10,000 investment in Cray Research—at the beginning of 1977—was worth $100,000 in early 1981.

But such gains pale when compared with those racked up by IBM and other high-technology stocks of the 1950s and 1960s. IBM, already a sizable company in 1945, nevertheless made fortunes for faithful holders thereafter. Those who bought and retained stock costing $10,000 in 1945 were worth $1,900,000 by 1970. But $10,000 worth of Xerox purchased five years later, in 1950, before the company developed its revolutionary copiers, was worth $5,558,000 in 1970.

Relatively few investors were shrewd enough to capitalize on this post-World War II high-technology boom. Many tried to hit the jackpot with Sperry Corp., General Electric, and RCA—all mainframe computer builders once believed to be nearly as promising as IBM. Their shares did little, though. It was years after the computer was invented before it became obvious that IBM had the necessary marketing skill to insure the success of those who invested in it.

Most investors do not realize that the finest technology will not guarantee important stock market rewards for the investors. The company also must be superbly managed in terms of the shareholders' interests—something that requires skills often lacking in high-technology companies, as we shall see.

Thus, while Sperry was the pioneer in mainframe computers, that technologically sophisticated company failed in its efforts to exploit the market. Sperry lost out to IBM with technology no better than Sperry's. In fact, some believe that IBM's computers while completely satisfactory were nevertheless inferior to Sperry's in those early critical years. IBM's superior management prevailed.

Picking and Choosing for Big Rewards

Unfortunately, in that earlier era there was no way of knowing which of the many companies that developed high-technology products would prove to be adept marketers and thus reward their shareholders. Individual investors had no objective tests for measuring progress that could be translated into stock market gains. By contrast, there are quantitative tests today—and this is critical:

Easy-to-apply tests can tell you when a company is growing and when it is beginning to lag. These become available to the general reader for the first time with the publication of this book.

What's more, the tests can be applied months, even years, before the investing public generally realizes that the game is over in particular instances. There is no other source presently available to individual investors of this vital profit-generating information.

Thus, this book will not only help you find the companies that are in the forefront of high technology, it will steer you to those companies that are managed well in behalf of their shareholders.

Yesterplays

Not only will this book help you avoid companies with limited prospects, it will also steer you away from yesterplays—the growth stocks of an earlier era that are still among the most coveted holdings in professional portfolios. Sometimes the professionals are slow to learn. Polaroid was a great stock ten years ago. But it is a yesterplay in terms of the relative saturation of its basic markets today. Most of the investors who rode Polaroid up to 150 in 1972 rode Polaroid back down to 15 two years later. The shares haven't seen 65 since.

It is important to realize that companies, like human beings, go through stages. They have an infancy, early growth, and maturity. They may live longer than humans but eventually they wither with age.

We are focusing on future stocks—those with a shot at sales and earnings at least ten times as large as today in just ten years time. When this happens, generally speaking, the investor can expect his shares to go up by a similar multiple.

This calls for real growth (inflation-adjusted) of 26 percent a year compounded—no mean feat but many high-tech companies are doing it and then some. And these high-growth, inflation-defeating stocks are the ones we'll be seeking out.

IBM may well enjoy a new beginning and extraordinary tenfold

Introduction

growth over the next ten years. But with current sales of over $25 billion, it would have to experience revenues of $250 billion, account for 10 percent of today's gross national product, to meet the criteria. Poignant as the professionals find it, IBM hasn't had much snap in the stock market for ten years. Essentially, IBM has stood still. The best hope for investors is that the Federal government will succeed in its attempt to break up IBM into a number of smaller companies so that the promise of a number of different high-growth prospects can be developed and the investors in each enriched. Some pros are counting on this, unlikely though the prospect is.

Remember: IBM is only the most prominent of scores of yesterplays that are unlikely to put you ahead of the pack—that is, earn you tenfold profits. Mostly, this calls for investments in companies of relatively small size. Many of the companies we'll discuss will have sales of under $250 million and a few as little as $25 million. We're looking for big game in terms of *market potential.* And we're looking for quality, for winners and not also-rans. Through the use of sales and value tests, we'll find them.

Mining Wall Street's Gold

From a stock market point of view, the timing couldn't be better for gains in high-technology stocks. The long-term sweep of the stock market is up. And a bullish environment for stocks generally will help high-tech shares reach their promise.

Robert Farrell, respected market analyst for Merrill Lynch, Pierce, Fenner & Smith, Inc., noted recently that real estate, commodities, and collectibles have had their bull phase. But stocks have not kept pace.

The cash-rich pension funds meantime receive $50 billion dollars of new money each year as corporations set aside money for their employees' retirement. Mr. Farrell believes the pension funds will be buying increasing numbers of shares, particularly in view of the fact that the prime alternative investment—bonds—experienced a "crash" in 1980, losing a third of their value in six months. Bonds plunged to even lower depths in the summer of 1981.

Such traumatic action in a major sector of the financial market tends to have a long-term effect, causing investors to turn their attention to other sectors of the market for "protection" and higher profits. (Investors bought bonds after the mid-1970s stock market crash.) As billions of new dollars seek out undervalued shares, higher prices inevitably must follow. Moreover, Mr. Farrell notes that in 1968 equities comprised 30 percent of individuals' financial assets. But by 1980 the figure had fallen to 10 percent of assets, the lowest level in at least 15 years.

Everything seems ripe for action and the most impressive action will be in high technology—one of the few sectors of the economy that is still growing by quantum jumps.

What's a Computer?

Here is another important factor in your favor as an investor: In the 1950s, when mainframe computers were just beginning to change the face of the business world, nobody except a few highly qualified electronic professionals knew what they were and what they were capable of doing. Even professional money managers bought shares of these companies on faith. But in the past few years, the word has spread. Today school children are training on computer terminals; and tens of thousands of workers are using them as routinely as they once used pencil sharpeners. Terminals are becoming as familiar a part of office nomenclature as the telephone, and most of us have at least a passing knowledge of them—we've watched others work with them or worked with them ourselves.

The great majority of investors now accept the fact that computers are the wave of the future and are focusing on this sector of the market. This widespread acceptance gives high-technology shares new momentum that will work for you.

Your Rosetta Stone to Riches

This book, then, can be your Rosetta Stone to riches through high-technology investing as an extraordinary new era of history unfolds;

an era the National Academy of Sciences calls the Second Industrial Revolution.

The author has drawn on 25 years of writing about finance for *The New York Times* in composing this book—15 years as author of the daily "Market Place" column, which frequently covers developments in high-technology shares. He has interviewed dozens of top executives of the foremost high-technology companies. He has sought out the most knowledgeable professionals in both high technology and the stock market to help you determine what works and what does not work when investing for profit in high-technology shares.

Follow the story, pick up the knowledge, and find the trail to the pot of gold. There is no magic to it. Finding wealth in Wall Street is merely a matter of study, care in selection, and, more generally, common sense.

We are not dealing with an ephemeral, transitional stage in American history. This movement is long term. It will last for decades. You do not have to worry about the short-term trends.

Golden Oldies That Paid Off

Well-chosen stocks have been making investors rich for decades. In 1971 there were 365 different securities valued at 100 times the prices at which they could have been bought four to 40 years earlier. That is, a $10,000 investment in any of those 365 stocks would have been worth $1,000,000 in 1971. Even adjusted for inflation, the investor who committed $10,000 emerged rich.

Obviously, many of these stocks were high-technology companies like IBM and Xerox. Where, then, are the IBM's and Xeroxes of tomorrow? This book will show you the way to the *Future Stocks* and help you find the way to financial independence in these uncertain economic times. Remember, after World War II, everyone expected a depression, and the atmosphere of gloom was palpable—just as it is today. Many lost ground financially. But others found financial security for life. Few imagined then that we were on the threshold of a vast new and important stock market era.

Now as then—in this gloomy period of skyrocketing energy costs as the quality of life erodes before our eyes—the alert can and will move ahead. The high-technology companies will lead the way. As investors we will have no one to blame but ourselves if we fail to capitalize on this new and exciting investment era.

PART I

ENTERING THE WORLD OF HIGH TECHNOLOGY

RARELY in the course of industrial history has a single device been so important to the future as the computer-on-a-chip. The Industrial Revolution of the eighteenth and nineteenth centuries thrived on cheap power. But the technological revolution comes at a time of even more costly fuel.

The computer-on-a-chip is remarkable because it takes almost no power at all. Therefore, it is uniquely suitable for this time. Those who sense this and invest in those companies which use these devices will be rewarded beyond their dreams.

1

The New High-Technology Revolution and Low-Cost Energy

CONCEPT: *The United States investor is looking for a few good stocks, to paraphrase a recruiting poster. It only takes a few to do the trick and they are not that hard to find. Remember that in the past generation 365 securities in a universe of 10,000 provided profits beyond the dreams of avarice. Thus, many investors who discovered and stayed with a handful of holdings like Xerox and IBM became financially independent. With the Second Industrial Revolution, this route to success will be swifter and more rewarding than ever before.*

There's an old chestnut about a young journalist who covered a raging flood in a distant valley community. In the aftermath, he telegraphed a story that began: "God sat on the mountaintop here yesterday contemplating the devastation he had wrought." The veteran editor who read that gushy first paragraph couldn't resist a withering reply. He wired: "Forget flood. Interview God. Holding four columns on page one."

The journalist's enthusiasm is understandable. Water on the rampage is awe-inspiring—but no more so than the turbulence of high technology today. In writing about it, there is a temptation to begin as effusively as an unseasoned reporter.

For the recent extraordinary outpouring of space-age products has already changed the way we live. Science promises to change our life styles and habits in even more dramatic fashion in the future, while improving our standard of living, although many of us have despaired of holding our ground in a world of limited resources.

Science even promises a solution to the central problem of the world today—shrinking energy supplies. The evidence clearly suggests that high technology will be instrumental in solving this problem once and for all early in the next century. It will do so through a variety of approaches that are startling both in overall scope and in individual significance.

Item: High technology is contributing greatly to our efforts at conservation of fossil fuels, which cost 10 times what they did when the Arab oil embargo of October, 1973, brought the reality of limited resources to our national consciousness. High technology has contributed substantially to the effort to convert our houses, offices, and factories from energy sieves to fuel-sipping, airtight boxes; our automobiles from petropigs to mechanical ectomorphs.

Enter the Fabulous Chip

Scores of manufactured items occupy important niches in today's high technology, but a single miraculous device, a sliver of silicon no broader than a collar button and called the microprocessor figures so prominently in the equation that it constitutes the foundation on which the high-technology revolution is being built.

Here's how the microprocessor evolved: In the beginning, there was the vacuum tube perfected for radio by Lee DeForest in 1906. It gave way to the transistor (invented in 1948) which was followed by the integrated circuit about 1965. Ultimately thousands of microminiaturized transistors were placed on a silicon chip through the process of photoreduction.

The Great Leap Forward

In 1971 a young Intel Corporation engineer named M. E. Hoff, Jr., made a giant leap in technology. He inscribed a computer's CPU, or

The New High-Technology Revolution and Low-Cost Energy 13

central processing unit—the "brain," as it were—on the silicon chip and then added two memories. One memory stores the data being processed, and the other programs the CPU. Mr. Hoff had invented the microprocessor, a device that eventually would cost a mere $10 though it packed the computing wallop of computers that had cost $100,000.

Happily from an investor's point of view, microprocessors were invented in this nation, and most of the important companies that make them and those that use them as components are American. That means we Americans are uniquely situated to capitalize on the boom. (We Americans, and the ever-present, ambitious Japanese, with their own highly competitive product.)

Sifting Sand

Here's what makes the microprocessor so important: Unlike so many key products of earlier eras—the steam locomotive and the dynamo, which, typically, were massive and costly to build—the microprocessor is tiny; and the raw material, essentially sand, is cheap. The cost of production is modest—modest, that is, once a company has spent the enormous sums necessary to get into the business in the first place. What's more, unit costs are still falling rapidly.

Tiny though microprocessors are, they are veritable powerhouses. The most advanced—Intel's newly developed "micromainframe" with three ¼-inch chips—contains 219,000 active elements yet is small enough to fit in a bread box. Astoundingly, the Intel device is equal in power to IBM's huge mainframes of years past. (The mainframe of a computer system is the cabinet that houses the central processor and main memory. The term mainframe has come to denote the larger all-purpose computer.) Though the Intel device works much less rapidly, the cost of the three-chip complex is, of course, miniscule in comparison to the IBM mainframe.

But the key breakthrough in circuitry came with the invention of the microprocessor itself. The salient point: One species of electronic circuit can be programed to handle any one of an endless variety of tasks.

The electronic ancestors of the microprocessor, the transistor and the integrated circuit, were capable of a single, explicit task. The versatile microprocessor is generally known for its ability to run a hand-held calculator. But that same single microprocessor can be programed to control city traffic flow by sequential changing of all local stop lights. A microprocessor of identical design can be programed to dispatch dozens of elevators for most-efficient building service. With different instructions, the same microprocessor can tell a ship captain how fast he can beat through storms of varying intensity without endangering his hull.

Such a microprocessor can be directed to analyze blood samples for a large health services company. Handicapped citizens take heart: Simulators powered by a microprocessor can give voice to those rendered speechless by paralysis of the larynx and can actuate an array of sophisticated controls in the paraplegic's home. From the viewpoint of the nation's marijuana smokers, consider this sinister aspect: Microprocessors are programed to sniff for marijuana concealed in luggage as it passes through the nation's commercial airports. Don't forget that the control of the fuel intake of most new cars is handled by a microprocessor—a multi-million dollar market.

Giant Steps into the Future

Remarkable though microprocessors are, their development continues to advance by quantum jumps. By 1986 a million active elements will be placed on a single chip—like legions of angels dancing on the head of an electronic pin.

The rate of advance in the state of the art is awe-inspiring. Of eight key manufacturing processes used to make today's microprocessor chips, only one process is over six years old.

Simply stated, the microprocessor and other computer-based marvels are fostering a second industrial revolution that is making the one that occurred in the eighteenth and nineteenth centuries seem as remote as the Stone Age.

We tend to forget how fundamentally things are changing in the present amazing age. Focus for a moment on the calculator. Twenty years ago, typewriter-sized calculators weighing 45 pounds and priced

The New High-Technology Revolution and Low-Cost Energy 15

at from $800 to $1,000 did our hard math by plodding, mechanical means—multiplying one number by another. Tens of thousands of these machines are still in service, though hand-held calculators weighing 3 ounces and priced at $15 can resolve with lightning speed complex calculations well beyond the capability of the old machines. The new calculators—in a marked departure—have memory capacity, so that interim computations can be stored and factored into later calculations.

The sleek devices are an everyday convenience for millions. They offer energy-pinching features, and their silent operation contrasts dramatically with the jarring clatter of the old mechanical machines. In place of heavy-duty wiring to grounded 110-volt outlets, today's hand-held models are powered by tiny batteries—some by solar energy even—and are thus as useful on the beach as in the board room.

Eniac to the Rescue?

Meantime, mainframe computers, still caricatured as behemoths in Walt Disney movies and newspaper cartoons, have actually undergone even more amazing shrinkage. In 1946, as the computer era dawned, Sperry Rand's Eniac weighed 60,000 pounds and was big enough to fill an entire floor in a skyscraper.

That pioneer computer, which Sperry built for the Army and then developed for commercial markets as Univac, was like a candidate for high office—power hungry. It drank electricity like a wattaholic—at a rate of 140 kilowatts per month. That's the equivalent of the power required to run 70 modern apartments.

Eniac employed huge, especially designed venting stacks to dissipate the heat of its thousands of vacuum tubes. By contrast, today's microprocessor weighs one ounce, consumes two watts of power and displaces little more than a cubic inch. The reliability factor provides even more dramatic contrast. Average time to breakdown for Eniac, a matter of hours; for the microprocessor, years. (A farmer discovered a lost hand-held calculator in his field not long ago. Despite the ravages of an intervening winter and the damage caused when a horse stepped on it, the durable device was still working.)

Consider cost: The Eniac cost the Sperry Rand customer millions of dollars. The typical microprocessor chip of today costs about $10.

Think about this shrinking price for electronic devices in terms of basic units. As recently as twenty years ago, a high-quality transistor cost $20. In 1979 the cost of an element in an integrated electronic circuit was 2 thousandths of a cent. That's a million to one price reduction in 20 years. Had the price of the Rolls-Royce dropped in similar fashion, it would cost $70, deliver 2,000 miles per gallon, and develop enough horsepower to drive the Queen Elizabeth 2.

That the price of electronic circuitry has continued to plummet in an era of double-digit inflation makes the accomplishment that much more remarkable.

Scientists and industrialists are so enthralled with the potential of the new microprocessors that they see them as the energizing force behind a boom that will change the face of the world.

Computational power is already so inexpensive, so convenient, so abundant, that consulting engineer and newsletter writer Benjamin J. Rosen calls the emerging era that of "free intelligence."

Number crunching—the prime function of computers in the past—is giving way to deduction. Writes Rosen: "The computer is beginning to emulate human thought processes and be involved in problem solving, planning, and hypothesis formulation. All these characterize machine intelligence. In turn, the availability of this free intelligence to consumers and industrial users means that entirely new classes of consumer and industrial products will be created, some of which we conceive of now and others which are still beyond our imagination."

Microprocessor Razzle-Dazzle

These ideas are meant to dazzle. For they are the fundamental facts underlying an electronic intelligence revolution. Let's compare the changes that are occurring with those of the earlier industrial revolution, which marked the end of the agrarian age and eventually spelled doom for that characteristic element of those slow-paced earlier times, the horse and buggy. The buggy whip, once as commonplace as flies in a stable, became a universal symbol of the passé.

The New High-Technology Revolution and Low-Cost Energy

That great movement took place between the middle of the eighteenth and the middle of the nineteenth centuries. In addition to changing dramatically the way crops were harvested and goods were produced, the industrial revolution urbanized society and upgraded standards of living enormously in both Europe and the United States, where key developments proceeded more or less simultaneously.

Initially, the industrial revolution produced such bellwether farm inventions as the steel plow, the mechanized reaper, the threshing machine, and the cotton gin. Spinning and weaving machines were developed to process textile fibers, moving yarn and cloth production out of the cottage and into the factory.

More fundamentally, the industrial revolution brought the steam engine for both railway locomotion and factory propulsion. In most respects, the revolution was energy based—depending largely on coal and later on oil and gas—the fossil fuels.

Low-cost power was the key. Our grandparents may be forgiven for claiming that indoor plumbing was the greatest advance of their era, but the period's most significant innovation was in fact long-distance transfer of energy by means of electric wires.

This brought safe, dependable electric lighting to rural households, extinguishing forever the kerosene lantern in all but the poorest, most remote areas of the land. Those same wires were to power electric motors to further mechanize our factories and to power, among myriad other devices, pumps drawing water from wells and milk from cows.

The New Age of Electronics Arrives

How can we mark the end of the industrial revolution and pinpoint the beginning of the modern age? The age of mechanics was essentially over when electricity, which had already brought forth the telephone, moved into a new and prophetic phase involving electronics. Electronics brought us wireless telegraphy and radio broadcasting—both employing the air waves.

The radio era began in the 1920s. Ever since, we have enjoyed major new electronic products periodically. Until recently, they came at a deliberate pace—one or two major products per decade.

The decade of the forties was marked by black-and-white television, while the fifties brought us stereo radio and color TV. The sixties brought us CB radio.

But continuing ferment in electronic laboratories began to translate into a burgeoning number of consumer products. Mainframe computer number-crunching was an early development, as we have seen. Computations that would take a talented mathematician a lifetime to complete were spewed out in minutes, the numbers coursing through transistorized circuits like lightning.

The Microcomputer as Superclerk

As the size and cost of computers shrank with the development of microprocessor materials, the amount and kinds of work they did burgeoned. The new "free intelligence" was to put the computer in the role of superclerk. The computer began storing and producing on demand facts that had been buried in filing cabinets, essentially irretrievable.

Consumers really began to experience the fruits of semiconductor research in the 1970s with the advent of the hand-held calculator, the digital watch, the microwave oven, the video cassette recorder, and the language translator. Thermostats were developed that ordered conditioned air according to outside temperature, time of day, and number of occupants in a home. Sophisticated electronic appliance controls were developed and so was the personal computer.

The pace accelerates. It is clear that new products will proliferate in the 1980s and 1990s as a result of ever-improving electronic technology—particularly in the technology of the microcomputer. As *New York Times* science writer Malcolm W. Browne expressed it not long ago, "The awesome memory and computating power of the new thumbnail gadgets can sift needles of scientific information from haystacks of noise—control factories, design complex machinery, predict weather and earthquakes, program wars and the national economy, find oil, and create still better chips. . . ."

Microprocessors will bring us electronic mail and electronic libraries, which we'll peruse with home and office computer terminals. With our morning coffee, we'll enjoy up-to-the-minute dispatches, as we "flick the pages" of an electronic newspaper displayed on a flat book-sized television screen. We'll be constantly in touch through cordless, dialable telephones tiny enough to make a phone booth out of a shirt pocket. Locks will open at the sound of the owner's voice—and blow the whistle on the most skilled impersonator.

Sun Power Does It Best

The microprocessor will help us tap the power of the sun—the basic source of all our energy. While it is fashionable to scoff at sun power as a dream of visionaries, our ability to capture its energy-laden rays is already more developed than many realize. To cite one example: Cal Tech scientists developed and flew across the English Channel recently an experimental solar-powered airplane. Wide-bodied jets powered by sunrays are out of the question for the foreseeable future, but the world's primary energy source provides the obvious route for supplying some of our basic needs.

The sun transmits more energy to the earth in a single day than is used by the entire world in a year. About 1 percent of this solar energy is permanently captured and stored by the earth's trees and plants, but even this small fraction is ten times greater than the world's total annual energy needs.

The Ever-Present Microprocessor

We've been extracting some of the energy stored in vegetation for centuries. Through microprocessor-aided genetic engineering, alteration of tree and plant fibers promises to produce considerably more ethanol for gasohol or straight use in automobiles than has heretofore been possible.

Self-Sufficiency in Fuel: Will It Ever Happen Again?

With the aid of microprocessor technology, the sun will someday heat and air-condition our homes directly. High-powered transmission lines—symbolizing the fullest flowering of the industrial revolution—will be diminished in importance.

Photovoltaics: The Second Miracle of Silicon

The photovoltaic cell—another silicon-based device of fundamental importance in high technology—converts sunlight directly into energy and promises a new era in household electrical use.

The potential of photovoltaic cells offers a marvelous example of the serendipity that can accompany technological development—serendipity that can help investors in high-technology stocks time and time again.

Consider this: Scientists regarded battery storage of excess energy generated by photovoltaic cells to be an almost insurmountable problem. Then someone remembered that the utility power grid works both ways. It can receive power as readily as it sends it out.

Thus householders can sell excess power to the local utility when more is generated than needed and buy from the utility when the sun goes down or when their photovoltaic cells are putting out insufficient power on cloudy days. Eventually this will help reduce imports of foreign oil, since the power company shuts down furnaces when household "payback" power pulses into the plant from private homes. At the end of the month the utility will net out each household and bill those that owe and send checks to those that have produced more than they have used. This two-way power flow is already occurring in some experimental roof solar systems in this nation.

Investment tip: The high-tech company that produces a photovoltaic cell at low cost promises to become exciting—particularly if a spin-off company is set up to exploit the development.

The Semiconductor as the "New Crude"

These high-technology developments and others equally significant promise self-sufficiency in energy and a new era of plenty. And the key element in the equation is semiconductor technology. Fortunately for investors in this nation, Americans are in the driver's seat—

The New High-Technology Revolution and Low-Cost Energy 21

uniquely placed to capitalize on this new industrial revolution.

W. Jerry Sanders, III, chairman of Advanced Micro-Devices, called semiconductor technology the "crude oil" of the electronic revolution. Consultant Benjamin M. Rosen focuses on the significance of Mr. Sanders' analogy in terms of American enterprise. He writes:

> Another aspect of the analogy is that both crude oil and semiconductors are becoming increasingly scarce commodities in terms of the number of companies capable of producing state-of-the-art devices. But the key difference is that where the OPEC nations have the crude oil, we have the newer crude oil—semiconductor technology.

Despite low unit production costs, very Large-Scale Integrated Circuits are so complex that only a few corporations in America and Japan are even in the race.

Whither Growth?

Semiconductor technology will spin off dozens of growth stocks in the future that will rival the IBMs and Xeroxes of past years.

Rosen predicts that the entire integrated circuit industry will grow from the present $5 billion annually to $80 billion by the end of the century, making the industry "not only one of the most important in the world but also one of the largest...." That would be equal to more than 3 percent of today's gross national product.

CAVEAT: *The integrated circuit industry is currently in depression. That's the bad news. The good news is that prices are sliding so fast that companies using integrated circuits are accelerating innovation at substantially lower cost.*

The age of high technology will be so fragmented and specialized, Rosen says, that production equipment previously designed and built in-house will be purchased from specialists better able to concentrate upon the specific requirements. Thus billions of dollars will fill the coffers of support companies in addition to the billions in revenues taken in by primary companies. And billions of dollars will flow into the coffers of companies that learn to employ microprocessors in useful products of their own.

The Era of Future Stocks

These developments have fundamental significance for investors. Already, the high-technology revolution has fostered opportunities in the stock market unequaled in a generation. In short, we are entering the era of future stocks—of a hundred high-technology companies whose shares will experience tenfold spurts in value in ten years or less.

Sharing the Wealth

Even prosaic non-computer companies with data bases like Dun and Bradstreet may become candidates for impressive stock market gains as they find new profits in old information resources.

For the computer scientists have brought the arcane world of information retrieval to the fingertips of the average employee. While businessmen may fret that the computer age has passed them by, it is a fact that anyone who can type—even by the hunt and peck method—can command computers and make them speak.

Computers are being taught to listen to and respond to English. Just so, those of us who man the keyboards need no familiarity with Fortran, Cobol, or other exotic machine languages to use the computer effectively in everyday tasks.

With a new language called "Intellect," the terminal user can communicate in conversational English (Americanese might be a better way of putting it). The MIT-developed system takes operator commands and makes "safe" assumptions about instructions given in colloquial English. Thus the user might type in the request: "Give me the names of all employees who live in Boston and Cleveland." The Intellect system would assume that the operator meant Boston or Cleveland, since the exact phrasing would produce no results. No employee, apart from a salesman in a Captain's Paradise, would live in both Boston and Cleveland.

The command "Tell me the average income level of all people who work here" would get this response: "Don't understand income level. Please substitute a synonym."

Answer: "Income level is salary."

At this point, Intellect would go to the memory file on payroll and prepare an average salary for all employees.

Harried non-programmers need this sort of help to feel comfortable working with computers. "Intellect" assumes no prior knowledge of machine language or of the contents of the memory bank. Experts believe that Intellect-type systems will soon break the software bottleneck that has restricted growth.

Cullinane, a leading computer software company, is already using Intellect in many of its customer installations.

True, it took math whizzes and computer programmers to make all this possible. But how many pianists can tune a piano? Even unskilled employees manning the keyboards of computer terminals can turn out work that will produce new sources of profits for non-computer companies and, in some cases, help put them in the supergrowth category—make future stocks of their shares.

New Markets for Old Companies

In sketching out the boundaries of the new electronics, let's examine the premise of computer-based profits for non-computer companies more closely—dramatize this unexpected route to stock market profits. Newspaper reporters now work on computer terminals. With this method of recording and storing facts, a newspaper like *The New York Times* or the *Washington Post* can go national, publishing the bulk of its daily news stories all over the nation. The computer doesn't care how long the umbilical cord—it will feed information by wire, microwave, or satellite to locations anywhere in the world.

As a result, national newspapers can be published at a fraction of the cost of local operations. Assuming skillful exploitation and further assuming that the market exists for such a journal, added profits could enrich the newspaper company's shareholders.

The semiconductor and the computer itself have invaded the nation's hospitals in myriad new life-support and analysis machines. Shares of producers of such equipment can become future stocks, too.

The dramatic increase in health care spending has given this field dynamic growth potential as Federal dollars by the billions flow into the coffers of companies that design and build laser-based microsurgery equipment and electronic patient monitors. Manufacturers of hospital accounting and billing machines—all computer-based miracles of modern science—may thrive as well.

The Highly Rewarding Quest for Values

Years of excitement are ahead for investors. Indeed, the coming years will be the most exciting ever for investors. Weigh this important fact: Investors are rarely able to buy shares of high-growth companies without paying dearly for the privilege. Therefore it is truly exciting that shares of many of the promising companies of tomorrow are selling at price-earnings multiples well below prices that became characteristic during the last generation of superstocks.

Prior-generation superstocks clearly illustrate the point. As the promise of mainframe computers unfolded in the fifties and sixties, investors were to pay up to $60 for a dollar's worth of earnings. That is, Standard & Poor's office equipment index carried a price-earnings ratio of 60, on the average, in the year 1961.

By contrast, a select list of computer-based high-technology stocks today would cost considerably less—even as little as $20 for a dollar's worth of earnings in some cases. The leaders are not all that cheap, of course. But some of the lesser known ones are. Thus, the stock market offers a once-in-a-lifetime opportunity as industry enters a new Age of Camelot.

The problem is to find the key issues in the years ahead. In some respects, this is easy. In others, less so. As technology changes, leadership also changes. Consultant Rosen notes that the vacuum tube industry in 1954 was dominated by a "big five": RCA, Sylvania, General Electric, Raytheon, and Westinghouse. Today, the semiconductor industry, which has largely replaced the vacuum tube industry, is dominated by new names: Texas Instruments, Motorola, National Semiconductor, and Intel among them. RCA, once one of the most promising electronics companies, Mr. Rosen points out, has become a high-tech dropout, with emphasis on conglomeration—through financial services, home furnishings, and car rental businesses, none of which are growing at anywhere near as fast a rate as the electronics field.

Household Names, Anyone?

Leadership in the semiconductor industry itself has changed. In 1958 the number two semiconductor company was Transitron and number three was Philco. Philco was acquired by Ford and has been phased out, while Transitron is not a company of major consequence today.

Some other leaders included Hoffman Electronics, Westinghouse Electric, Bendix, and Clevite. However, as Mr. Rosen points out, these companies are "not your household semiconductor names today."

Calculator industry leadership has also changed hands in less than a decade. Of the previously important electromechanical calculator companies—Friden, Marchant, Victor, and Monroe—none is now a major force in calculators. The big names today are Casio, Sharp, Texas Instruments, and Hewlett-Packard. In computer mainframes IBM still leads. But as this was written the other mainframe companies, Honeywell, Univac, Burroughs, and Control Data, were not important in personal computers—a major growth area. Instead we see Tandy's Radio Shack, Apple Computer, and Commodore and a late starter, IBM. Look for industry leadership to continue to change in the 1980s. This prospect of change calls for eternal vigilance—a willingness on the part of investors to admit mistakes and to replace disappointing holdings.

Thus the search for future stocks is not duck soup for the amateur stock market chef, but a delicate soufflé calling for a balance of investing skills. You'll have to be watchful and thoughtful. But you won't have to be a math whiz.

Remember that some of the most successful investors never experienced the new math. Nor do they have extraordinary intelligence. In point of fact, many of the savviest investors are average people with no special investment expertise. For Wall Street's Camelot and its future stocks are there for the ambitious no matter where they went to school. It is even there for dropouts who have learned in the school of hard knocks. It's catching the right wave that counts in the stock market—and on Wall Street, too.

SUMMARY: *The revolutionary microprocessor—the computer on a chip—has sparked a new industrial revolution. Some investors have already grasped the significance of the new technology and have made fortunes on shares of companies in the technological forefront. But the stream of riches is only beginning to flow. The bulk of the market gains are still in the future.*

This is no pipe dream. Key industry figures are calling the microprocessor "the new crude oil" to emphasize its strategic importance in the world. They note that America—hotly pursued by Japan—leads in microprocessor development, which continues at a blistering pace. In short, America and Japan are the microprocessor haves, while the rest of the world including the oil-rich OPEC nations and even sophisticated Europeans are the have nots.

American manufacturers of the microprocessor itself, American companies that use microprocessors in computer manufacture, and some American companies that employ computers in place of typewriters and calculators will enjoy exploding earnings. Share prices of the winners will rise in tandem with earnings of the companies themselves and become future stocks. Those who latch onto the concept of the new industrial revolution and buy shares of the best companies will prosper and, assuming canny investments of as little as $10,000, can become rich.

2

What Is Growth?

CONCEPT: *Companies that persistently chalk up earnings gains of 26 percent a year will post similar gains in the stock market. At that rate, share values will rise tenfold in ten years' time. This assumes that the company's return on invested capital remains high relative to inflation. Even with an adjustment for double-digit inflation, a $10,000 investment worth $100,000 ten years hence is a big winner.*

The "T. Rowe" Way to Go

Before his retirement some years back, T. Rowe Price was a Wall Street original. Irascible and egotistical, he did not work easily within an organization—even his own. If a colleague in his own company outperformed him in the market, Mr. Price would compete ferociously, seeking not only to surpass the upstart but also to humiliate him.

But Mr. Price was so adept at investing in rapidly growing companies and so articulate about his work that professional investors still look to him for guidance. What's more, his methods, which brought him success for more than 40 years, are as valid today as they were when he developed them.

Mr. Price loved to illustrate how well the investor could do with relatively modest gains—by doubling invested capital every ten years.

In making his point, he employed the so-called "rule of 72." That rule says that money growing at a 7.2 percent rate compounded annually will double in 10 years.

Mr. Price looked to put together an entire portfolio that would provide that kind of earnings growth. That is, he had to find some big winners whose growth was substantially more than 7.2 percent to outweigh the shares he picked that experienced growth at substantially lower rates. He exceeded that goal over and over again during a half-century investing career. He assumed that market values of the shares of the high-growth companies would grow apace. But he qualified this. The earnings growth rate would certainly have to be over and above any increases in the cost of living. (In this era, then, earnings growth would have to be considerably higher in order for real value to double every ten years.)

If real (inflation-adjusted) growth continues at the 7.2 percent rate, things get better as time wears on. During a 20-year period, the value of a portfolio progressing at that rate would increase by over 300 percent and in 30 years it would increase by over 700 percent; in four decades by 1,500 percent.

But that kind of growth is far less than we are seeking. Assume for the moment that you found a relatively small high-technology company that grew at an inflation-adjusted rate of 15 percent—a little better than twice as fast as that called for by the rule of 72. This is an attainable rate for the stocks we'll favor in this book. Compounded at that rate, invested capital would increase by more than 300 percent in a ten-year period, and by more than 1,500 percent in 20 years. In 30 years it would increase by more than 6,500 percent, and in 40 years by 26,686 percent.

We'll be looking primarily at companies that show a rate of growth even greater than this—but not for 30 years, of course. Because at that rate and by that time the company would be gigantic. (Or maybe it would be IBM.) In any case, Mr. Price invested in many companies that grew at better than a 15 percent real rate, shares that thus made a massive contribution to his efforts of at least doubling his investors' capital each ten years.

"Avon Calling!" Recounting a Fabulous Stock Market Success Story

For example, Price purchased shares of Avon Products at the equivalent of $0.875 a share in 1955. Those shares were worth over $136 a share at the end of 1972. This is an increase of 15,528 percent, or a compound annual growth of 34.6 percent. The dividend paid in 1955 was 0.04 cents and in 1972 it was $1.35. This is an increase of 3,275 percent, or a compound annual growth of 23 percent. Now we're talking. To repeat: We'll be looking for high-technology shares tending to match Avon's record in those 17 glorious years.

Growth-stock investing requires patience. But the buy and hold approach reduces worry, frustration, brokerage commissions, and capital gains taxes.

Remember that during a 20-year period of supergrowth between 1950 and 1970, the Standard & Poor's office equipment stocks—the shares in which growth was most concentrated—shot up from a base of 20 to over 1,500. That's an increase of 75 times. Meantime, the S&P index of 400 industrial stocks went from 20 to 80—a mere 4 times and a fraction of the distance covered by the office equipment shares.

The promise of rewards even a fourth as great as the office equipment stocks provided in those 20 years would be enough to dazzle any red-blooded investor today. And this spectacular performance of the past should be repeated in the years ahead. Already things are popping.

Hambrecht and Quist, a San Francisco brokerage house specializing in high-technology companies, notes that its supervised list of 75 high-growth companies recorded annual earnings growth averaging 32.1 percent compounded for the five years ended 1979, and 40 percent for that final year, 1979. The list showed a 54.4 percent appreciation in share price in 1979, and still the shares traded at average price-earnings ratios of 12 to 15 times. They've gone to higher PEs since, but they are still attractive.

To emphasize a point: Remember that such shares are also relatively volatile. Temporary dips should be ignored—high-growth shares

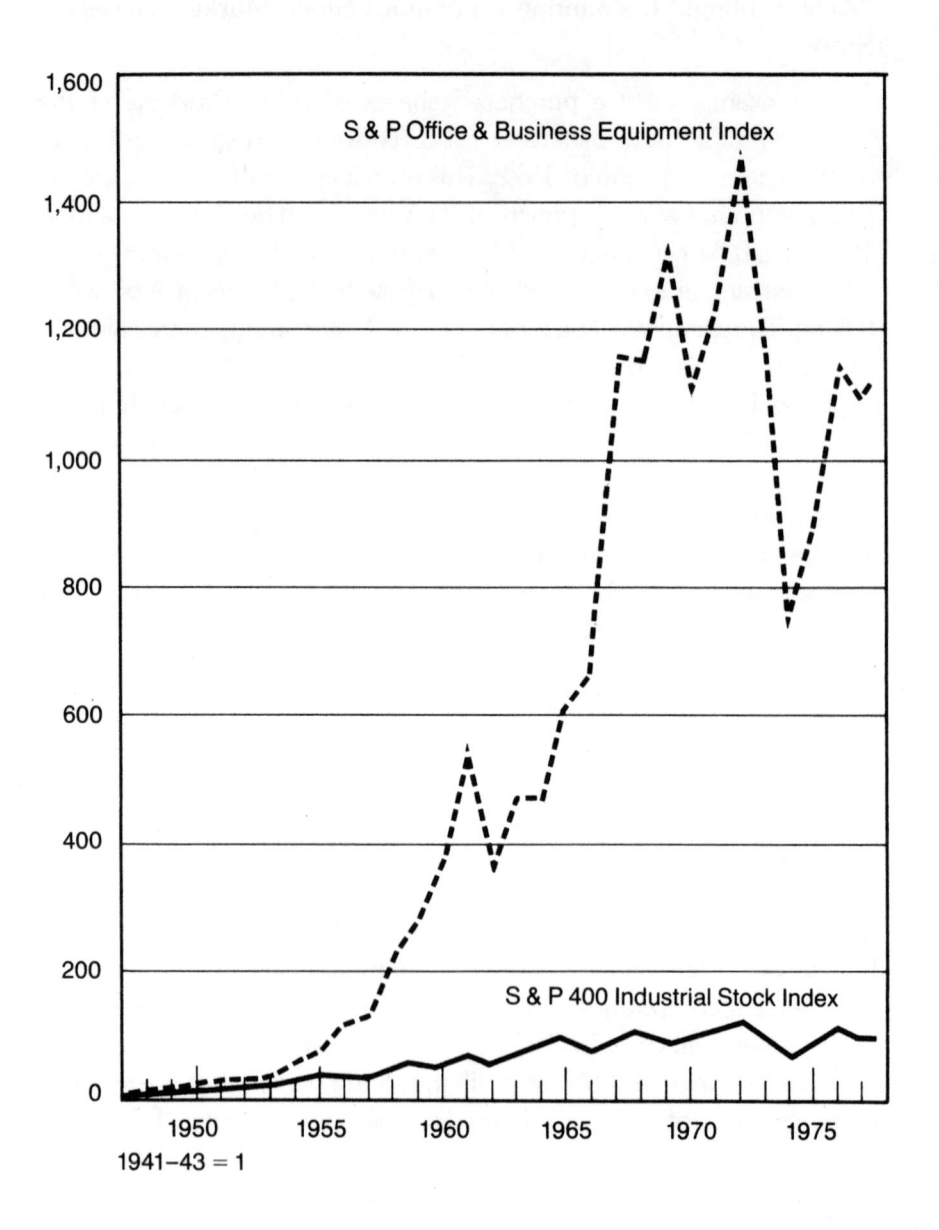

Entering the World of High Technology

S & P Office & Business Equipment Index

S & P 400 Industrial Stock Index

1941–43 = 1

What Is Growth?

must be held for the long term if the investor is to reap full benefits. When the investor is sure of his ground, dips may be regarded as buying opportunities.

The Quarter-Million-Dollar Bonanza Club

Over the past decade a $10,000 investment in shares of any of 77 companies listed on the Big Board or American Stock Exchange could have led to gains in excess of $250,000 by the end of the first quarter of 1981.

Gains in a few of these issues came quickly indeed. For example, the high-technology companies Rolm Corporation and Wang Laboratories racked up gains of about a third of a million dollars in just five years. Prime Computer produced a bigger gain—over $550,000 in a shorter period.

(In fact, Prime Computer did even better than the list on pages 32–33 suggests, with a gain of at least $800,000 over a slightly longer period. Obviously, the list has certain shortcomings, but in every case gains of at least 25 times the investment are clearly indicated.)

Commodore: The Ultimate Winner

Now hear this: In six years, a $10,000 investment in Commodore International, Ltd., the home computer maker, would have brought a $1,765,200 reward.

While the table makes the unrealistic assumption that the money was invested at the ten-year low and that the shares were sold at the ten-year high, except for a few cases, it wasn't necessary to catch the low and high in order to rack up the contemplated quarter-million-dollar gains.

That is, shares usually trade at or near a low point for some weeks, and highs also persist, so that the investor can sell without undue haste if the company's deteriorating circumstances should require this. Thus, an investor who had chosen his stocks carefully and held them while fundamentals were positive would still have been able to chalk up the quarter-million-dollar gain during the ten years.

Entering the World of High Technology

The Quarter-Million-Dollar Bonanza Club

Name	Where Traded	Date Bought	Date Sold	Appreciated Value at $10,000*
AVX	N	12/31/74	11/30/80	$325,930
Acton Corp	A	12/31/74	11/30/80	461,430
Adams Russell	A	12/31/74	3/31/81	743,060
Advanced Micro-Devices	N	1/31/75	11/30/80	359,910
Alpha Industries	A	12/31/74	3/31/81	627,830
American Agronomics	N	11/30/76	3/31/81	500,000
American Medical International	N	9/30/74	12/31/80	293,100
Arrow Electronics	N	9/30/74	11/30/80	262,760
Astrex, Inc.	A	12/31/74	9/30/80	452,130
Baruch Foster	A	8/31/74	11/30/80	261,360
Best Products	N	12/31/74	8/31/78	349,430
Caesars World	N	12/31/74	6/30/79	560,000
Cenvill Communities	N	11/30/74	11/30/80	274,850
Charter Medical	A	12/31/74	3/31/81	859,090
Commodore International	N	12/31/74	12/31/80	1,715,520
Community Psychiatric Centers	N	8/31/74	3/31/81	277,960
Computervision	N	12/31/75	3/31/81	752,290
Crystal Oil	A	11/30/71	3/31/81	335,780
Datapoint	N	12/31/74	12/31/80	389,740
Delhi International Oil	A	9/30/75	3/31/81	564,420
Empire, Inc.	N	12/31/74	12/31/80	313,410
Esterline	N	12/31/74	11/30/80	281,350
Felmont Oil	A	8/31/74	11/30/80	262,400
First Mississippi	N	4/30/73	11/30/80	300,570
Flightsafety International	N	8/31/71	3/31/81	457,080
Flow General	A	10/31/74	12/31/80	1,000,000
Forest Laboratories	A	10/31/74	3/31/81	353,170
GCA Corp	N	11/30/74	12/31/80	691,440
Gearhart Industries	N	6/30/73	11/30/80	681,820
Gerber Scientific	N	12/31/74	11/30/80	944,440
Guilford Mills	A	12/31/74	3/31/81	291,180
Health-Chem	A	12/31/74	12/31/80	481,330
Houston Oil	A	11/30/72	3/31/81	556,370
Humana	N	9/30/74	3/31/81	628,810
Integrated Resources	A	11/30/74	11/30/80	295,070
Kirby Exploration	A	9/30/76	3/31/81	320,920
Lennar Corp	N	12/31/74	3/31/81	263,740
Lifemark	N	11/30/74	3/31/81	289,100
Litton Industries	N	12/31/74	12/31/80	320,870
Loral Corp	N	12/31/73	11/30/80	440,000
M/A-Com	N	9/30/74	12/31/80	331,240

What Is Growth?

The Quarter-Million-Dollar Bonanza Club (con't)

Management Assistance	N	9/30/75	8/31/78	525,000
Materials Research	A	12/31/74	11/30/80	502,430
McMoRan Oil	N	4/30/75	11/30/80	278,110
Miller Wohl	N	6/30/74	8/31/80	379,870
Mitchell Energy	A	4/30/75	11/30/80	392,070
NVF	N	6/30/71	1/31/80	320,000
National Education	N	12/31/74	10/31/80	523,570
National Medical Enterprise	N	9/30/74	3/31/81	435,000
Nexus Industries	A	12/31/74	3/31/81	362,930
Pall Corp	A	11/30/71	12/31/80	393,940
Petro-Lewis	A	12/31/74	11/30/80	1,042,890
Prime Computer	N	1/31/76	12/31/80	557,430
Pulte Home	A	11/30/74	3/31/81	462,120
R H Medical Services	A	12/31/74	3/31/81	270,830
Resorts International	A	12/31/74	9/30/78	1,271,840
Resorts International	A	12/31/74	9/30/78	1,512,410
Rolm	N	10/31/76	12/31/80	343,750
Rowan Companies	N	4/30/71	12/31/80	274,390
Safeguard Industries	N	12/31/74	3/31/81	447,740
Sanders Associates	N	12/31/74	11/30/80	288,890
Scientific-Atlanta	N	12/31/74	3/31/81	502,320
Scope Industries	A	9/30/72	12/31/80	457,140
Shearson Loeb Rhoades	N	8/31/74	12/31/80	551,470
Tandy Corp	N	12/31/74	3/31/81	478,000
Teledyne	N	11/30/74	3/31/81	418,990
Texas Pacific Land Trust	N	11/30/71	11/30/80	269,520
Tracor, Inc.	N	12/31/74	3/31/81	352,680
United Energy	N	8/31/74	11/30/80	275,960
United National	A	11/30/75	2/28/81	362,600
Veeco Instruments	N	12/31/75	11/30/80	325,270
Wainoco Oil	A	12/31/74	8/31/80	490,000
Wang Laboratories (B)	N	5/31/76	12/30/80	328,000
Western Company of North America	N	8/31/74	11/30/80	460,310
Whittaker Corp	N	12/31/74	3/31/81	308,910
Wichita Industries	A	11/30/73	11/30/80	316,670
Woods Petroleum	N	8/31/74	11/30/80	317,670

N—New York Stock Exchange A—American Stock Exchange
*The publicly owned A shares. The other listing is for the B shares, which are convertible into A stock on a one-for-one basis.
Dividends if any are not included in any of the totals.

SOURCE: Computer Directions Advisors, Silver Spring, Md. The values indicated are for the end of the month and are based on ten years' experience unless trading information was not available for that period of time. In some cases, therefore, gains may have been higher than indicated, but in every case the high was at least 26 times the low. Data believed to be reliable but have not been verified on a case by case basis.

Note that the list includes a number of crude oil producers—about a dozen—which the author regards as special cases reflecting the extraordinary hikes in crude prices resulting from OPEC agreements over the past several years.

But there are far more future stocks of the sort discussed in this book than oil producers—such as electronic and computer companies, oil equipment, office equipment, and hospital management companies. By and large, these high-technology companies depended on management skill to a greater degree than did the oil producers.

The author contends that major gains in high-technology shares are more predictable than those in most other industries represented by this list. More important, the bonanza in high-technology shares is only beginning. Find yourself some future stocks and make your fortune. (See pages 32–33 for table.)

Buffett on the Elusive Nature of Bargains

Keep this in mind: In concentrating on future stocks, you'll find that price-earnings ratios are generally higher than for the rest of the market.

Certainly many investors who resist stocks with price earnings ratios above 10 wouldn't think the Hambrecht and Quist stocks are cheap today. They'd rather look for bargains at four times earnings.

Warren Buffett, one of the most respected professional investors at work today, isn't interested in bargains. He is chairman of Berkshire Hathaway, a textile company that makes a great deal of money through Mr. Buffett's investments in the shares of other companies. He comments from sad experience on his efforts to make money in stocks purchased at bargain prices. A bargain, he says, is rarely a bargain. He shuns "turnarounds" at low price-earnings ratios. Turnarounds are companies with serious problems that speculators conclude will be solved for great profit to themselves. Mr. Buffett prefers to pay the high price-earnings ratios associated with highly profitable businesses. He comments:

> In some businesses . . . it is virtually impossible to avoid earning extraordinary returns. . . . And assets in such businesses sell at equally extraor-

dinary prices . . . reflecting the splendid, almost unavoidable, economic results obtainable. Despite a fancy price tag, the "easy" business may be the better route to go.

In this instance, Mr. Buffett was speaking of the high prices commanded by network television stations—not our kind of future stock, but his rule regarding price applies to future stocks nevertheless. Once a high-technology company has joined the magic circle of highly successful companies, a high share price is justified because, given superior management, a track record, and continuing research and development, its chances of further success are substantial.

What Then Are the Growth Stock Criteria?

Ralph Kaplan, growth stock analyst for Brean Murray, Foster Securities, Inc., lays out a series of "prime requisites" of a true growth company:

1. The company has shown a consistent growth pattern and should continue to be able to do so.
2. It can finance its own growth out of retained earnings.
3. It has dominant market positions, and high margins relative to its competitors.
4. It is well managed.
5. It has premium product lines, i.e., most of its products are leaders in their fields.
6. It has the ability to create its own growth because of its strong franchises, rather than being at the mercy of market forces.
7. In addition, the company enjoys some advantages which are of particular relevance in a highly inflationary economy.
8. Finally, the company will be one of the major beneficiaries of rapidly advancing computer technology.

Would you believe that in laying out these parameters Mr. Kaplan was writing about McGraw-Hill? Once again, this is not the sort of stock the author is singling out—except in born-again growth companies. Mainly, I am talking about high-technology companies that are well established yet relatively young. Mr. Kaplan grants that no company need fit all the criteria, but argues that a true growth company will meet most of them. His criteria are helpful guidelines in evaluating potential high-return future stock companies.

The Magnificent Leveraging Effect of Debt on Future Stock Profits

Some experts take exception to Mr. Kaplan's point number 2, arguing that debt incurred to finance a promising new product can lead to far greater growth than otherwise would be possible in some cases. (See Intel story page 00.)

The important thing is that debt be kept within manageable limits. Pre-tax profits should be at least three times interest expense, that is, a company that borrows $10,000,000 should report pretax earnings of at least $30,000,000. Looked at another way: Be suspicious of companies whose capitalizations are more than 35 percent debt.

Contrariwise: Avoid Companies with Heavy Short-Term Debt

Interest charges on short-term debt are pegged to the bank's prime lending rate—that rate charged the bank's most creditworthy business customers.

The prime rate has fluctuated all over the lot in recent years, and charges on short-term debt fluctuate with the prime. It is one thing to borrow money at 12 percent, quite a different thing to borrow at 20 percent. (The prime rate went from 12 percent to a record 21.5 percent in a three-month period ending December 19, 1980.)

Besides, most banks require the corporate borrower to keep part of the money borrowed on deposit at the bank in non-interest bearing accounts. Thus, at a nominal 20 percent borrowing rate, the corporation with a "compensating balance" of 20 percent actually would be paying 24 percent.

The long-term debt market has been hostile since 1979. This is because many avid holders of long-term bonds have been scared off by

What Is Growth?

rising interest rates, which cause the value of existing long-term bonds to fall. To wit: When interest rates go up, the price of outstanding bonds drops until the new price offers a yield equal to that available on new bonds of similar quality. Oversimplifying somewhat, a long-term bond priced at par (100) to yield 10 percent ordinarily will drop to about 80 if yields on new bonds of similar quality are priced to yield 12.5 percent. Therefore, a $5,000 bond bearing interest at 10 percent would drop to about $4,000 in a 12.5 percent market. But there is a road to credit uniquely open to high-tech companies. The financing method—convertible debentures—allows investors to participate in high technology by entering through the back door as it were.

The Investor's Back Door Entry to Low-Cost Future Stocks

Convertible debentures offer a back door entry for investors seeking outstanding high-technology shares.

While the convertible debenture offers the investor an interest yield somewhat lower than pure bonds, holders receive the right to buy shares in the company at a preset rate. Assuming the company uses the convertible issue proceeds well, the debenture holder eventually will be able to obtain his shares at a discount.

The convertible debenture holder might, for example, be able to turn in each $1,000 debenture for 20 shares of stock for an indicated price of $50. The shares might well have sold at $40 at the time the debentures were issued and later moved to $60. At the later point, the investor would be able to buy in at a $10 a share concession to the stock market—a savings of $200 per $1,000 debenture.

Two high-technology standouts, Wang and Prime Computer, have used convertibles well (to offset the effects of inflation) in recent years, and holders have obtained a call on their shares at attractive prices. Recently Intel pleased believers in convertibles by offering $150 million of the securities, thus borrowing money in the public market for the first time. Keep an eye out for convertible offerings by future stock candidates.

This is a ploy uniquely suited to investors in fast-growing companies.

Most high-tech companies using this low-cost means of raising equity capital have done exceptionally well in terms of profits and—of fundamental importance to investors—in terms of rising market valuation of the company's shares.

The Outsider's Inside Information

Some argue that a company's future spending plans can be uncommonly revealing. While such information can be as valuable as restricted knowledge known as "inside information," it is readily available in many cases. In fact, a company's future spending plans are not restricted information at all. Management is free to talk and is generally eager to tell all who will listen about the golden future it foresees and the capital it is spending to bring that future about. Once the investor has picked a high-technology company for investment, he would be wise to contact management and ask about future spending plans.

Robert Campbell, president of a New Jersey investment counseling firm called Investors Security Services, Inc., contends that information about corporate spending plans is often available 12 to 24 months before the fact. And to get to the core argument, he insists that companies with heavy spending plans usually have the best prospects.

He offered this example of what big spending can mean: In 1978, Analog Devices, a manufacturer of connectors for measurement and control systems in computers, doubled capital outlays to over $12 million. This spending program was an enormous one relative to the company's share price. The spending amounted to $2.25 a share. In early 1978 the stock traded at 8½. The plant and equipment investment in that one year therefore represented a quarter of the entire market value of the company. Mr. Campbell comments: "Obviously, Analog Devices was going to fly or crash. As it turns out, management was right and within two years the shares, which trade on the Big Board, were selling at about 24."

Is this a surefire method? Mr. Campbell has had more winners than losers, but concedes that sometimes management's heavy spending plans represent a mistake.

Mr. Campbell said that investors who chose to employ this concept should do several things: They should attempt to find out whether the corporation's competition regards the added capital spending as appropriate. Even individual investors find that they can reach the sales manager of a rival company and get the needed information in many instances.

Mr. Campbell said that the investor should also find out one way or another how management intends to finance heavy new expenditures. This may be apparent from the annual report or it may be announced. If it appears that the spending program will raise the company's debt-to-equity ratio to significantly more than, say, 50 percent, it may well be that the risk overshadows the potential appreciation.

Mainstream High-Tech Profit Generators

Let's take a brief look at one of those smaller, high-technology companies in the forefront of the computer revolution. The story of Intel is typical of future stocks and of the exceptional growth we seek in such stocks. Intel is one of the leading designers and manufacturers of semiconductors. Determined not to fall behind in a flat-out technological race, Intel, like many other high-tech companies, spends about 10 percent of sales for research and development. As you know, Intel produces semiconductors on small chips that perform complex electronic functions. Its success has been remarkable when one realizes that a little over a dozen years ago Intel didn't even exist.

The company was incorporated on July 18, 1968, and on October 31, 1971, Intel raised $8 million in an underwriting. Growth since then has been phenomenal by any measure. Over the past five years, sales have grown at a rate of 39.5 percent compounded. In 1980 the company's revenues reached $855 million. Meanwhile, earnings have soared at a 34.5 percent annual rate of growth. No dividends have been paid. But who cares? Intel has provided the kind of growth we are seeking—and then some.

Dividends are for companies that cannot put the money to work in the business in a manner designed to support rapid growth.

That is, dividends are for older, more mature companies. Few future stocks offer dividends, so such shares should not be purchased for income. Shareholders attuned to the high-growth concept do not complain about a lack of dividends, and they don't complain about Intel. The stock has been split on several occasions and shares have increased in value by 1,800 percent; a $10,000 investment at the underwriting price would have grown to $180,000 by mid-1980 (based on the median price of the shares during the period January 1 to mid-May, 1980).

There is, of course, no guarantee that the company won't slow down or that it will continue to be in the forefront. In fact, 1981 was a disaster for Intel and other similar companies.

In the investment-strategy section, we set forth methods for monitoring high-growth companies that clearly show when they are beginning to lag—years before most investors become aware that this is happening.

In any case, during the past ten years at least, Intel has been the kind of company we will look for in the years ahead. Intel has been the kind of issue that can be called a future stock.

As investors, we'll be attempting to set up portfolios that contain as many Intels as possible.

Mutual Admiration Societies

You don't necessarily have to pick your own future stocks. Some readers, once the future stock concept is understood, will prefer to seek major market gains in high-technology shares through the purchase of leading mutual funds designed to ferret out rapidly growing companies—high-tech companies for the most part. Once you understand the future stock con-

What Is Growth?

cept, you can succeed either way. Either way, the rewards may be nothing short of sensational, though direct investing done well should lead to superior results since there will be no dilution by non-high-tech shares.

Among the mutual funds which seek out aggressively growing companies, here are the ones that have performed best over the past five years. (These funds manage at least $10 million.)

	Through March 31, 1981		
	Year to Date	3 Years	5 Years
Twentieth Century Growth Fund* 605 W. 47th Street Kansas City, Mo. 64112	0.5%	321.5%	468.6%
Hartwell, Leverage Fund* 50 Rockefeller Plaza New York, N.Y. 10020	−1.6	243.2	292.6
44 Wall Street Fund* 150 Broadway New York, N.Y. 10038	−0.8	189.9	287.8
Value Line Leverage Growth 711 Third Avenue New York, N.Y. 10017	10.7	126.8	285.0
Pace Fund 2777 Allen Parkway Houston, Tex. 77019	11.7	161.8	284.9
Security Ultra Fund 700 Harrison Street Topeka, Kan. 66636	−6.3	220.7	276.7
Constellation Growth Fund* 331 Madison Avenue New York, N.Y. 10017	−1.5	267.5	268.7
Weingarten Equity Fund* 331 Madison Avenue New York, N.Y. 10017	−2.5	201.6	267.1

OTC Securities Plymouth & Walnut Avenues Oreland, Pa. 19075	3.0	126.8	259.6
IDS Growth Fund 1000 Roanoke Building Minneapolis, Minn. 55402	4.6	219.1	246.2
Standard & Poor's 500 Stocks	1.4	78.2	68.8

*No-load funds—that is, funds can be invested in directly and without selling fees. The figures are from Computer Directions Advisors of Silver Spring, Md. 20910, which notes that all figures presume reinvestment of all distributions.

SUMMARY: *We are focusing on future stocks—those with a shot at sales and earnings at least ten times as large as today in just ten years' time. When this happens, generally speaking, the investor can expect his shares to go up by a similar multiple.*

This calls for growth of 26 percent a year—no mean feat, but many high-tech companies are doing it and then some. And these high-growth, inflation-defeating stocks are the ones we'll be seeking out.

PART II

ZEROING IN ON PROFITS

Introduction: The Road to Riches

The companies in this section of the book are beautifully orchestrated enterprises. Finely tuned, they are as outstanding in the ways of business as the New York Philharmonic is in the art of playing classical music. Each of these high-technology businesses has done extraordinarily well. But the divergent ways in which they have achieved their success demonstrates clearly that many roads lead to Eldorado.

No one can guarantee, of course, that these great companies will continue to excel. They may. There will certainly be winners in the group. But remember that these companies are to be used by you, the reader, as indicators of methods that work for specific kinds of high-technology companies.

Let the Author Be Your Proxy in the Executive Suite and in Wall Street's Inner Sanctum

Individual investors are sometimes frustrated when they seek interviews with executives of the most important high-technology companies. And some Wall Street firms place barriers between individual investors and their top company analysts. In 25 years of covering finance for *The New York Times,* the author has crossed those barriers many times.

"Information, Please"

In high technology as in sports, you can't tell the players without a program. You're going to need information and lots of it to make a reasoned investment decision.

Fortunately, critically important information on well-established companies is readily available. Chances are a high-technology company will come to your attention through the pages of this book—or as a result of an article in the financial press.

Once you have a line on a company, write for its annual report.

In reading the annual report, use the Oriental method: Read from back to front. Beware of the promotional letter to stockholders. Start in the back with the footnotes, which will clue you into any major shortcomings. (The expression "buried in the footnotes" evolved naturally.)

Ask the company for that somewhat more detailed document, the so-called "10-K" report. All publicly owned manufacturing companies are required to keep 10-Ks on file with the Securities and Exchange Commission and to forward them to shareholders requesting them. Some high-tech companies with progressive public relations programs fold their 10-Ks into the annual report. Companies that won't send annuals or 10-Ks are suspect.

There are a number of services that offer investment assessments of high-technology companies. See the *Value Line Investment Survey,* which reviews on a single page each of a thousand of the nation's most important companies. The service places more emphasis on high-technology companies than do some rival services like Standard & Poor's *Stock Guide* and Moody's *Investors' Service.* But those two are useful, too, and are widely available in business libraries. All these services can be obtained through subscription.

Value Line is at 711 Third Avenue, New York, N.Y. 10017. Standard & Poor's Corp. is at 25 Broadway, New York, N.Y. 10004. Moody's Investors' Services is at 99 Church Street, New York, N.Y. 10007.

> Datapro Services offers a wealth of marketing information on technology companies. It is available in business libraries, where helpful related publications can be found.
>
> Don't hesitate to call a company for information. (Ask if there's an 800 toll-free number on your first paid call.)
>
> Remember that high-technology companies are seldom approached directly by shareholders. Yet the best ones welcome such contacts.
>
> Personal contacts with local companies may be exceedingly helpful to you—once you know the basic situation.
>
> Get to know a junior executive in each of the high-technology companies in your area that seem promising. You can find out all kinds of things through informal contacts. Consider taking the junior person to lunch: an assistant treasurer knows everything you need to know but isn't as busy as the boss. He or she will be flattered, and eager to help.

We shall try to convey insights to successful company management that are rarely available outside of Wall Street. In other words, the idea is to give the small investor something that is hard to come by—some added tools with which to make intelligent investment decisions about the nation's fastest-growing companies.

Readers will discern characteristics common to highly successful companies—fundamental qualities without which any enterprise, however promising, can be expected to lag. For example, a company with a unique product and exceptional marketing skills can always borrow money to finance its growth. But if it borrows so much relative to its capital that interest costs tax its ability to cover expenses, it may not survive. What's more, without clever, experienced management, no company, however promising the product line, can hope to achieve rapid growth and high profit.

Discovering Those Winning Techniques

Generally, the companies in this section have restricted their borrowings to less than 35 percent of capital and most of them have borrowed even less than that. Different managements have taken different tacks and have still emerged in the exceptional group.

The author has attempted to identify both common characteristics and special ones so that the reader will be able to spot promising situations in terms of both the usual and the unusual. Thus, Advanced Micro Devices is identified as a well-run company that emphasizes employee incentives as a means of earning high profits. Conversely, Intel Corporation is labeled as a well-run company with solid financing that spends large sums on research relative to the competition—and so it goes.

It will also be apparent that the author has singled out types of companies that are most representative of the new era of high technology. Note that the companies discussed do not represent all types of high-technology companies—do not represent all the categories of companies whose shares could be regarded as future stocks. The personal computer software companies, the companies offering video games, and companies offering advanced forms of office automation equipment get short shrift or no shrift at all though all these are highly promising areas.

Every book must have limits or it risks becoming a catch-all with no coherent message. My idea, then, has been to set forth a general message with as many specifics as possible and with no attempt to be exhaustive. It is up to the reader to apply the lessons to his own future stock candidates. If I have been successful, the guidelines should be clear.

OBSERVATION: *The investment strategy section offers tests of high-technology success that can be applied to industries which are not discussed in the book itself.*

3

Microprocessors: Nucleus of Change

CONCEPT: *High-tech core companies. Microprocessor companies produce the basic equipment for the new age of technology. As you might expect, then, the best-run companies in the field offer basic lessons for investors in future stocks and candidates for portfolios, too.*

For these and other reasons, two microprocessor companies are covered in considerable detail in this chapter—at greater length than most companies discussed in this book. Intel is one kind of story. Advanced Micro Devices, which emerged later, is yet another.

The Classic Start-Up

At one time Intel represented the classic, high-risk start-up situation, and it will be discussed first in that context. This is important, for most investors at one time or another are tempted to buy stock in enterprises at the time they offer their first public shares.

The Start-Up of Genentech

Before treating Intel in depth, let's consider risks to the early-bird investor. Let's consider Genentech. That high-technology genetic engineering company's early stock market performance offers stark evidence of the risk entailed in jumping in early—especially so when a company has gotten so much flattering attention in the press that share price already discounts an extraordinarily optimistic future.

Most investors who sought shares of this budding genetic engineering company were forced to buy in the aftermarket. That is, too few shares were included in the first public offering to meet the exceedingly heavy demand. Many bought shares within hours of the public offering and yet paid a heavy penalty for tardiness. These latecomers bought their shares from the lucky few who were alloted them by brokers. Many of the fortunate ones resold their shares for a quick, tidy profit. Offered initially at 35, Genentech reached 89 in the aftermarket the very day the shares were first marketed to the public, long before management's profitmaking talents were adequately tested. The price was excessive even if Genentech proves to be the Rolls-Royce of gene-splicing, as some expect it will. Share price soon fell to about half the high of that first day's trading.

For those who bought Genentech at or near the high on that first day, losses have persisted. At the beginning of 1981, the shares were still trading in the mid-30's. No profits from operations yet.

The Ruinous Fad Stock Syndrome

Fad stocks are dangerous and must be avoided at all costs. You have to be exceptionally careful, even when dealing with companies having great potential. A lofty share price may discount the earnings of the next couple of decades. Don't listen to Wall Street touts, let the company (through its financial statements) show you a track record—exceptional earnings and growth prospects. You've got time to make your killing. Move in after the air has cleared, after the fad followers have bailed out. It will happen—possibly after a bad year, inevitable for most companies. Thereafter, your golden opportunity to buy at a reasonable price may have arrived. Rule of thumb: avoid the stocks of new classes of companies for five years after the first company in the group goes public.

Obviously, the hazards of buying into young companies are enormous. Occasionally, though, something so unusual comes along that

Microprocessors: Nucleus of Change

the high risk may be acceptable. (This may even be true of Genentech at current prices.) But if you should decide to take a flyer, it may be months or even years before you know that you have guessed right. The Intel story will demonstrate clearly the critical importance of experienced management in a young high-technology company—something even the brave who insist on buying start-ups cannot ignore.

Intel: Little David Sidesteps the Giants

Intel was uncommonly blessed. The principals had been associated with each other virtually throughout their careers. They had gone through two earlier start-ups and, since they had faced the pitfalls of start-up before, knew how to avoid those pitfalls. The key element in Intel strategy was to avoid a head-on encounter with entrenched competition. To do so, Intel developed a new product for which no market had existed.

Intel's story is also instructive in terms of management's imaginative solutions to the peculiar problems of a high-technology business—particularly in terms of management-training techniques and response to the chaotic pricing conditions characteristic of high-technology markets generally. Here, then, is Intel.

Intel: Take Three

The first start-up experienced by the innovative scientists who founded Intel Corporation was at the Shockley Semiconductor Laboratory. The second was with a semiconductor unit of Fairchild Camera. Intel's founders, Gordon E. Moore and Robert N. Noyce, were the key people at Fairchild along with a group of fellow defectors from Shockley; Dr. Moore was research director and Dr. Noyce general manager. They quickly built Fairchild Semiconductors into a $150 million enterprise. In doing so, they acquired additional management skills that were to help them sidestep disaster at Intel.

Dr. Moore is chairman of Intel and Dr. Noyce vice chairman. Dr. Moore granted the author an extended interview and told what things were like at the time he and Dr. Noyce founded Intel. He emphasized as he did so what a tremendous advantage it was to have the prior experience of the start-ups. (To draw a parallel in an unrelated field, let us argue that a parachutist would have to be brave indeed to pack the parachute used in his first jump.)

What Dr. Moore says has relevance for investors scouting promising young companies of every stripe. His words have special meaning for those who favor high-technology companies. For in high technology, Intel is a latter-day IBM—a storybook company of the genre.

In a remarkably brief period as business goes, Intel has become a giant with 14,300 employees and 1981 revenues estimated at over $825 million.

The company has grown in large measure due to the premium it has put on hard work and creative dissent. Intel encourages its people to innovate and to defend new ideas against the criticism of the best brains in the company. The most junior members of the team can challenge the leaders, something that is seldom done in the structured world of established business. And these circumstances exist in an atmosphere of shirt-sleeve informality.

The Hard-Nosed But Informal Atmosphere for Innovation

Informality is hardly synonymous with a lack of boundaries at Intel nor with an unwillingness to hold employees to account. Dr. Noyce expects people to work hard. "We expect them to be here when they are committed to be here; we measure absolutely everything we can in terms of performance."

This approach might seem difficult in the management of scientists, but it isn't at all, Dr. Noyce told the *Harvard Business Review*. Scientists are used to being measured, he said:

> You know the old story about the scientist is that if you can't put a number to it, you don't know what the hell you're talking about. Well, as an example, customer service is poor—how poor? Let's measure what the response time is when a letter comes in and we'll plot that versus time. Let's measure how many commitments on delivery schedules are met, how many are met in a week, how many are more than a month late. . . . High

achievers love to be measured, when you really come down to it, because otherwise they can't prove to themselves that they're achieving.

The fact that you are measuring them says that you . . . care. Then they're willing to work—they're not only willing but eager to work in that kind of environment. We've had people come in who have never had an honest review of their work. We get senior managers who come in, and we say, "Okay, in your six-month review, or your annual review, here are the things that you did poorly, here are the things you did well." A lot of these people have never heard that they ever did anything poorly. It's the new culture of our schools, you know, no grades. Everybody passes. We just don't happen to believe in that. We believe that people do want to be praised so we try to do that. . . . They get their M&M candies for every job, as one of our business instructors always said.

Clearly the atmosphere is charged despite the fact that the interaction of the staff and the uniform of the day are casual. It is an atmosphere that has brought Intel extraordinary results—credit for Intel's young engineer, M. E. Hoff, Jr., as inventor of the computer-on-a-chip.

Thriving Silicon Valley

Intel, by dramatically advancing the art of computer-memory and the microprocessor, has grown enough in a few short years to match giant corporations that have been in business for generations. Operating in California's computer heartland widely known as Silicon Valley, the Santa Clara-based corporation is already an enterprise of international scope. Intel has offices in Brussels and Tokyo. Its factories hum in such corners of the earth as Barbados, Malaysia, the Philippines, and Israel. In 1980 Intel ranked 336 on the Fortune 500 list. In 1982 Intel seems sure to join the ranks of the nation's billion-dollar corporations, when its revenues should easily exceed those of the company that spawned it—Fairchild Camera. Intel already has 3,000 more workers than its progenitor and usually its profits beggar those of Fairchild, which has been acquired by Schlumberger. More important, from an investor's point of view, Intel's shares, split many times, have made some early supporters financially independent.

In short, Intel's extraordinary success in the dozen years of its existence is the talk of Wall Street, though the company hadn't gotten around to listing its shares on either the American or New York Stock Exchanges in 1981.

But Intel is already big enough that some are saying Intel's shares have had their day. Others predict that Intel, the sole source of some advanced products, will continue to enjoy exceptional stock market advances in the years ahead. This much is clear: Even with today's revenues, Intel is still small enough to experience the kind of growth IBM racked up in the late 1950s, growth that saw IBM increase several times in value. Whether that happens or not, Intel's experience is worth looking at as an archetypal high-technology growth company.

Start-Ups: Not Habit-Forming Perhaps, But Certainly Instructive

Gordon Moore is soft-spoken. He impresses a listener with the measured words of a scientist. He said in an interview with the author that he and his colleagues started Intel confident that they had learned at Shockley and Fairchild how to make a success of a start-up.

Intel's guiding premise: It is important that a new company have an idea that is different. Obvious though this may seem, many new companies make the mistake of picking a product that already has been established in the marketplace. As a result, the new business faces fierce competition in addition to all the other problems that stymie new businesses. Advanced Micro Devices chose to barge into established markets anyway and succeeded, as we shall see, but it still follows that "It is hard to jump in where other companies are already established," as Dr. Moore puts it.

After careful study, Dr. Moore and his colleagues concluded that they could advance computer technology dramatically in one sweep and thus establish a major new market. Reviewing Intel's efforts in the context of semiconductor technology, Dr. Moore said that in the 1950s computers were constructed out of simple transistors used as "logic gates" that had to be connected together to produce a complete computer circuit. By the early 1960s integrated circuits had come along and computers used them by the thousands. Says Dr. Moore: "We wanted to build them bigger. But as these devices were

Microprocessors: Nucleus of Change 53

made more complex to serve computer functions, individual integrated circuits became unique—usable only in a given computer application."

Intel wanted to print circuits that could be sold to users for disparate functions. He notes that the technology existed at the time Intel was formed for building complex computer functions, but it was then hard to see what functions could be built in a large repetitive manner that could be used universally. "At the time Intel started, we identified semiconductor memory as the function we thought could be adapted to get around this problem."

Computer memory is fairly broadly applied. Thus, a memory chip could be sold to a variety of customers for use in a variety of functions, or so it seemed to Intel scientists. Up to that time the memory function was handled magnetically by so-called magnetic cores. Each core was unique—not adaptable for use in other computer applications.

Dr. Moore says that the universal semiconductor memory "was the origin of our idea. It was a different idea—a way to get established and compete with larger companies by producing something they hadn't visualized."

For a start-up company a major plant with hundreds of workers is a nightmare. But, Noyce, Moore & Co. had settled on an idea with great appeal from that standpoint in that it did not require a big plant. Older computer memory system methods required labor-intensive assembly activities, while silicon chips, which Intel would use, were "silicon-processing intensive and less assembly-line intensive—no transistors to interconnect."

Dr. Moore and his colleagues saw this as an opportunity for developing their entrepreneurial plan on a basis that would utilize brainpower in place of factories. At the time, he said, there were a "lot of possible variations in the technology. We chose to use some variations that were never in production before."

The Luck of an Idea

Intel might have made a number of costly false starts. But luck played a role, says Dr. Moore:

We made some fortunate choices—things that worked out well beyond what we could have hoped for. The particular technology we chose—silicon-gate metal oxide semiconductor (m.o.s.) technology—had just the right degree of difficulty associated with it. We concentrated all our energy on solving the two or three major problems that were associated with the silicon approach. We were able to get over those difficulties fairly rapidly. We came out with our first products in about 14 to 15 months. It took our competitors—Texas Instruments and other established companies—much longer.

The Right Technology for an Exploding Market . . .

To paraphrase Shakespeare, Dr. Moore dost not protest enough. Intel's decision to travel the m.o.s. route to semiconductor success is regarded in scientific circles as a strategic move of fundamental importance. Other companies were attempting to develop similar devices but weren't sure which technology to use.

Intel was smart enough to put all development effort into m.o.s. technology instead of wasting effort on alternate technologies that seemed to offer higher speeds and better performance characteristics. Intel realized its m.o.s. technology would put the company into far more markets than any of the other developing technologies and would result in substantially larger unit volume over time. Its m.o.s. technology would therefore be cheapest—cost advantages would offset somewhat less than optimum performance characteristics.

. . . and Prices to Match

Semiconductor people generally use "experience curve pricing," cutting the ticket rapidly as the company learns how to produce at ever-lower cost. Experience curve pricing keeps potential competitors off balance; besides, a company that keeps its price high to skim the cream may earn less in the long run, as a premium price can bring unwanted competition.

> Let's assume that a semiconductor company produces an innovative item costing $200 a unit on the first one million produced. When cumulative production reaches 2 million units, the cost should come down in constant dollars by 30 percent. Thus, in this example, once the 2 millionth unit is reached, the unit cost would be $140. Produce a total of 4 million and unit cost falls to $98. Produce 8 million and the unit cost becomes $68.60. At 16 million, unit costs are down to $48.02. Turn out 256 million and the unit cost would be $10. As a rule of thumb, the unit cost of most semiconductor items drops to $5 pretty fast—sometimes by the third or fourth year of production. This works in other fields, too, but there aren't many markets for 256 million units using materials of little intrinsic worth.

The fact that large companies didn't race Intel in its chosen technology was not only providential but probably inevitable. Big companies, Dr. Moore said, "can't turn around in a hurry. They have too many things to protect. A small company can concentrate all of its efforts on one new product—there is no existing business to protect." Meantime, a competitor like Texas Instruments must devote considerable research and development effort just to maintain market leadership position in other product lines. Dr. Moore said that Texas Instruments could not take its ten best people and direct their efforts toward the development of one new product line. Large companies simply have "too many other things to do."

As a result, Intel had several years with its new memory devices "expanding into a vacuum." Intel was fortunate that it managed to solve the problems of technology as quickly as it did, considering the fact that company scientists couldn't know how difficult it would be to solve them. Dr. Moore says that if it had taken Intel three years to complete its work, Texas Instruments "might have beaten us to it." Or, Intel might have run out of money and had difficulty financing further research. It was also fortunate that Intel was never underfinanced, Dr. Moore said:

> We always raised money before we needed it. Remember that in 1968 (the crest of one of the most speculative bull markets in modern history) it was very easy to raise capital. My wife had people calling her at home to put in money. We had to ration it. From the beginning we planned on being a fairly large company. We never had to scrape through with a level of investment we thought less than necessary.

Dr. Moore makes it sound as though luck is a critical element in his company's success, and he clearly implies that other start-ups must have considerable luck as well. Perhaps that's a fair assessment of the importance of luck. After all, Napoleon didn't fire his generals because they were bad generals but rather because they were unlucky. Still, all the luck in the world won't help an ill-conceived enterprise or a badly managed one, and Intel was neither jerrybuilt nor mismanaged.

On the Importance of Management

In fact, Intel was superbly managed in nearly every sense. This is the key, and deserves elaboration for insights into what works in high technology.

The people chosen to begin Intel were hand-picked to fill big jobs. Says Dr. Moore.:

> We started with a group of people we thought would be capable of running a large organization—at 40 we were the old men of the group. They were all bright high-potential people. This is important. In my view, a startup is the ideal time to train managers. It is the only time for would-be managers to observe the entire business when the elements are simple enough that they can really understand all of them. It is much more difficult to develop a manager later on when the company is bigger and he cannot see the elements. We had the advantage, then, of training management right. Most of them are still with us and are in key positions.

But the Peter Principle played a role. Dr. Moore said that in a company growing as fast as Intel, it was sometimes necessary to promote before the individual was ready. When a man flounders under those

Microprocessors: Nucleus of Change

circumstances in other companies, he will probably be demoted and, crestfallen by his failure, leave the organization. But this is not characteristic of Intel, Dr. Moore said. He then spoke of "Peter Principle Recycling":

> We have tried not to make it a stigma to demote a man or woman and let that person come up in a smaller job. We assume the individual will catch up and eventually reach the higher job. This has worked well and has helped morale. We've found that our people recognize the problem before management does. I can think of one corporate vice president we had to do that with twice and today he is one of our most valuable guys.

Innovating for Profitable New Markets

Stressing the importance of inventions in Intel's success, Dr. Moore said that management came out of a research and development background and was comfortable working with new technology and "even products for which a market didn't yet exist. Our products have created their own markets."

Explaining the importance of the microcomputer, which Intel introduced about 1971, he said: "This was a complete computer on a chip that could do essentially anything because you could program it as you pleased. Thus we had a standard complex product that would do many things and for which a wide customer base could be developed."

The new product would do many things that were too expensive to undertake before. First there was a family of scientific calculators. Dr. Moore said that while this application is not too important now, it was critical then. He mentioned the use of the microprocessor in traffic light controls, in elevator dispatch, in blood analyzers, and in the marijuana sniffer. Data processing in general benefitted most, of course, and this was the most important application.

The "Exploding Market" Syndrome

With so much brainpower on board, Intel found unique solutions to some of the problems of innovating in an exploding market.

As indicated earlier, the price of computer products goes down nearly continuously, and this could destroy distributors with substantial inventories purchased at out-of-date prices. Of necessity, then, the manufacturer must protect the distributor against price declines and allow the distributor merchandise return privileges. Dr. Moore explains how Intel handled this problem:

> We set up a scheme whereby we don't recognize as a sale anything that the distributor hasn't sold to the ultimate customer. On our books, it is like it is still in our inventory. The IRS makes us pay taxes on the sale anyway, [but] we don't have to give [the distributor] credit for decreased prices because we've never charged him [the old higher prices] or taken the sales into book.

Meantime, Intel's inventories get overvalued as prices continue to fall.

> We put in some stringent inventory reevaluation procedures for our internal housekeeping. Having learned from experience, we knew we could prevent [adverse] things from happening [in the accounting sense] by using different systems.

Innovation for the Future

Intel's new micromainframe computer-on-three-silicon-chips includes an imbedded operating system that simplifies programing. Already tests indicate it will increase programer productivity by 800 percent.

Some believe this new product line will make Intel "the $10 billion company it ought to be," as an admiring analyst comments. It may also make Intel a future stock for some years to come.

CAVEAT: *Intel's management may not have served shareholders as well as it has served technology.*

Some say an Intel decision to finance growth internally was tantamount to forfeiting share of market to domestic and Japanese competitors.

Remember that Intel created and dominated the semiconductor memory market until 1974. But by 1977 Intel lacked sufficient productive capacity to meet the demand for memory chips. In 1977 the Japanese jumped in to compete with then current 16 K random access memory (RAM) chips. Since Intel didn't have enough 16 K RAM chips to serve the burgeoning market, it couldn't slash prices to slow the invasion. This would have been effective, as the Japanese chips were then inferior to Intel's.

Memory-related products were—and still are—Intel's largest and most important product area, with such sales fluctuating between 70 and 80 percent of total revenues in recent years.

To some, this was a tragic event in the life of Intel. In 1973 Intel's after-tax return on equity peaked at an astonishing 39 percent. It has since fallen to 22 percent. Return on investment might have continued at a much higher rate if domestic competitors and the Japanese had been thrown back at Silicon Valley.

Intel's earnings dropped over 90 percent in a recent quarter as a result of overcapacity in microprocessors and consequent price-cutting. Remember that investor sales can constitute a buying opportunity.

Nevertheless, a falling level of return on equity is a Wall Street negative that discourages aggressive accumulation of shares as it suggests share price growth has peaked or at least reached a plateau.

Why Debt May Be Essential

Observation: Judicious use of debt by rapidly growing companies, particularly for those in competition with the highly leveraged Japanese, may be necessary for proper exploitation of markets.

Critics argue that during the last half of the decade of the 1970s, Intel could have afforded to use debt extensively. Some believe an unusually high ratio of one dollar of debt for each dollar of invested equity would have been both prudent and affordable under the circumstances. Intel's exploding earnings would have supported this level of debt easily, and its use could have kept return on equity in the high 30s.

What Might Have Been

Here's how debt might have worked hard for Intel.

Assume that Intel had borrowed a sum equal to its investment in the business in 1975 and at a 10 percent cost. Assuming that Intel would have paid corporate taxes at a 50 percent rate, its net cost would be 5 percent on this debt. Assume further that Intel's return on investment was 22 percent and remained at that level. Subtract the 5 percent net cost of the borrowed money and the return on that part of the invested capital would be 17 percent. Add that 17 percent to the 22 percent that Intel earned on the equity portion of its capital and we get an overall return on equity of 39 percent.

For every $10 borrowed, Intel would have earned an additional $1.70 (17 percent) for its shareholders. By the way, Intel would have covered its debt four times in the example given. That is, for every $10 borrowed, the pretax interest cost would have been $1 and the pretax earnings would have been $4.40.

Those who believe Intel should have followed this course and thus kept the Japanese at bay also believe that Intel might have traded as high as 150 today compared with about 23 at press time.

A higher share price would have resulted because the increased use of debt would have accelerated investment and almost doubled the rate of earnings-per-share growth. In addition, the higher return on equity would have approximately doubled the price-earnings multiple of the stock.

Intel may have another chance for explosive growth with its 64 K RAMs — once the bugs are eliminated — and its new micromainframes. It's a good sign that Intel recently issued $150 million in convertible debentures.

Ideology in High Technology

Advanced Micro-Devices and its ebullient and highly talented president, Jerry Sanders, are illustrative of the role of ideology in high technology. While ideology is rarely important in the success of a run-of-

Microprocessors: Nucleus of Change

the-mill business, high-technology companies may offer a special case.

Overachievers—scientists and engineers—are often the guts of a high-technology enterprise. Inspiring them to leaps of brilliance is a key task—that and earning their loyalty. How to do it? Money talks, and never more persuasively than for the articulate Jerry Sanders. When he launched Advanced Micro-Devices a decade ago, he saw to it that every employee got shares, with hourly workers getting theirs free. Incentives are usually more generous in high-tech companies than elsewhere in business.

In all, 10 percent of pretax profit is earmarked for employee benefit plans. That sends AMD employee costs well above those of high-tech companies generally, but the dollars spent on employee morale have to be among the most important the company spends apart from those devoted to R&D.

Two Key Strategies for High-Tech Profits

1. *Superior product.* Sanders invaded the microprocessor market with a superior product that became the one to beat—the standard against which other companies' devices were measured.

2. *Selecting the right market*, Sanders sold his microprocessors as components in computer, communication, and instrumentation devices—the professional market. He shied away from the consumer market and its boom-bust economics.

Jerry Sanders: The Dream Merchant

"Net earnings for fiscal 1980 exceeded the cumulative net earnings of our first decade." Those words of Jerry Sanders occupy a space of an inch by an inch and a half on the stark gray cover of a recent annual report whose main visual interest is eighth-inch borders of red, yellow, chartreuse, and magenta.

The overall effect is surprisingly pleasing and reflects in a single image both the understated dress and the colorful style of the man. Sanders is, as we used to say, a fashion plate. He favors softly figured shirts with shoulder loops as a fillip, subdued ties and solid-color gabardine slacks. His round, youthful face is set off by the gray of his artfully trimmed hair and mustache—a gray generally associated with somewhat older men. There is a shine to his countenance as though lit by an inner fire. If so, it is the inner fire of a missionary.

An Important Ingredient for High-Tech Success: Environment

In fact, Mr. Sanders sees AMD as a "classical American Dream Company," having committed himself to the principle that all he need do is provide an appropriate environment in which overachievers can realize their dreams. Do that and big success will follow, though the innovation that results may produce on a delayed basis—like asparagus, an AMD symbol.

Asparagus has a long gestation period: "You cannot automate the harvesting of asparagus because the spears do not grow at uniform rates." But over time ideas will germinate and develop if AMD provides the proper climate.

Unsinkable by Doing the Unthinkable: Winning with Superior Product

And indeed a great success has followed, as that tease on the annual report cover shows. Like Intel, AMD makes microprocessors using metal oxide semiconductor technology. On other devices AMD uses bipolar technology. With both MOS and bipolar, AMD has succeeded in a big way. From the beginning it has done so by doing the unthinkable: marching into markets dominated by competitors much larger than AMD. At least, the competing companies once were much larger than Advanced Micro-Devices.

Not long ago, Mr. Sanders reviewed the progress of his decade-old company for New York security analysts. He offered them a prediction that sales would more than double from the $225 million level achieved in the year ended March 30, 1980. They'll reach a total over $500 million in fiscal 1983, he boasted. Profits, he added, will proceed apace in fiscal 1983 at a predicted $50 million, fully taxed.

Up AMD and the Industry Too

To reach the $225 million sales level, AMD grew "substantially in excess of the corporate objective of 30 percent compound per annum." In the March 1980 year, pretax margins rose to 16.5 percent, the highest in five years, while research and development expenditures were a record 12.5 percent of sales. Return on average equity for the year was 33 percent.

The picture is equally impressive when AMD is compared with the other companies in the industry. Mr. Sanders insists:

> Over the last five years, of the publicly held semiconductor companies, AMD has been first in compound growth in sales, first in compound growth in earnings per share, and for the most recently completed year, first in return on equity.

Recently he lectured the New York Security Analysts about the sometimes maligned industry—and, knowing that his remarks would be published, he was talking to Doubting Thomases generally. Mr. Sanders acknowledged that rapid price reductions and boom-bust production rates were inherent to the industry. But, he said, those who viewed those factors as exemplifying immature management are "ignorant of the dynamics of our industry.... The *raison d'être* of our industry is cost reduction. Central to the historic growth of our industry has been the reduction of cost and improvement of performance in electronic equipment made possible through advancing semiconductor technology."

He went on to tell the analysts:

> Expanding the central theme of the future growth scenario is a plethora of new products whose feasibility is only possible due to ever-lower cost solutions through advancing semiconductor technology. Therefore, fundamental to our industry is the concept of supplying ever more for ever less. . . .
>
> [Semiconductor technology is] the new crude oil that will fuel economic growth in the 1980s and beyond. . . . The companies controlling that technology should experience superior growth in sales and earnings over the next several decades.

A glance at cold statistics clearly suggests that Mr. Sanders has the manpower to row to victory across perilous waters. Advanced Micro-Devices does have long-term debt—but only $7 million of it, a mere 5 percent of capital. AMD had 6,632 employees at the end of the last fiscal year, and they were obviously among the best-paid people in America, by design. Advanced Micro-Devices spends an impressive 35 percent for labor. That relates back to Mr. Sanders' theory about building a great company with employees who share in the overall success. He explains to the author:

Rocketing to the Stars on Dream Power

The American dream is that everybody can improve his or her economic condition by working hard. We have programs so that as the company prospers, the people prosper. We were the first company in Silicon Valley to set aside 10 percent of pretax profits for employees. This goes to them half in cash and half in a long-term account as an incentive to stay.

Sanders argues that most companies only allow top management to participate in the equity ownership. By contrast, "We wanted every employee to be an owner." There is a restricted stock program under which all employees are able to buy shares periodically at prices 15 percent below the market. Second, under a separate plan all employees apart from hourly laborers were able to buy stock at "very favorable prices." One would have to agree that the price was favorable—the employees paid only 5 percent of the price paid by outside investors. AMD gave each hourly worker 250 shares which, after two splits, would amount to 600 to 700 shares each, Sanders said. "We gave them that stock as an incentive to become a part of the team. We wanted everyone to be an owner." Those who kept the free shares would be worth $25,000 on the basis of the AMD freebies alone.

Mr. Sanders stoutly defends the logic of these programs. He commented by telephone that, "I believe that a lot of people pay lip service to the idea that when people work hard and are productive, they can improve their economic conditions." But at AMD, it isn't lip service, but bona fide shares and coin of the realm that deliver on that idea, he said.

Doing It the Hard Way

The real gamble taken by Sanders and company was to take the AMD gun—organized with a modern plant and $1,505,000 in capital—and aim it at the established markets of considerably larger competitors.

> We started as an alternate source. We offered . . . replacements for what others were making. We were told that this guaranteed failure. "What are you selling, knock-offs?" our critics asked. Actually AMD produced a superior product. In 1970 [at the outset] we offered customers a superior level of quality to anything available from other suppliers. Everything was built to "mil" standard . . . all products were processed to achieve the level mandatory for military precision. No one else has done this before or since.

Mr. Sanders indicated that the idea wasn't original, noting that the Japanese have used superior quality as their means of conquering markets—as their entry vehicle—in every product they've introduced here and in other foreign markets since World War II.

Elaborating on his theme, Mr. Sanders said that

> Our strategy was that we would not introduce products except for markets that were oriented toward improving productivity. Such markets as that for computation, communication, and instrumentation devices. Therefore we were not involved in electronic wrist watches, calculators, CB radios, TV games, etc. [They were all boom and bust products, he noted.] We focused purely on professional markets. Why? These markets are more oriented toward quality products. You are able to sell them advanced technology because they are prepared to pay the price for that; they are interested in the total cost of ownership rather than just the price of the item.

He spoke of building professional equipment for customers like Western Electric.

> They want it to last a long time because costs are high. Total cost of ownership is a lifetime cost.
>
> Our devices would work in the same application as the products we were replacing—but offered superior characteristics. We are a semiconductor manufacturer. We don't make resistors, a field in which there is no product differentiation. There is by contrast tremendous product differentiation in semiconductors. Others had already established the market and our superior quality for plug-in devices helped us succeed.
>
> Our superiority might mean higher switching speeds, for example. So the end-use computer would then have more safety factors.

Speaking by analogy, Sanders said:

> If I give them a tire that won't blow out unless it is driven at 150 miles an hour, the safety factor is greater than with a tire that blows out at 100 mph. The engineering mentality wants that kind of margin. That's because there is more of a safety factor in the [end product] equipment.

Superior Products Set the New Higher Standard: Bye-Bye Blackbird

Over time, superiority pays off abundantly—when the customer begins to take advantage of AMD's superior performance. That is, under new specifications established by the customer based on the performance of AMD's components, the competitor's product no longer does an adequate job.

Sanders believes AMD has become the technology leader with proprietary products that represent state-of-the-art technology. Clearly, AMD has managed to wrest market share from competitors with this technique and has become highly profitable along the way. That in itself makes Advanced Micro Devices formidable and, for investors, a potential future stock. If it continues to enjoy major stock market success, it no doubt will reflect Sanders' enthusiasm, his vision.

"Money Is the World's Report Card"

At the end of the telephoned interview, Sanders returned to his basic theme: that happy, well-rewarded employees are the key to success.

> What has kept us going is improving the economic condition of our employees. Our people can get rich here.
>
> [But] we attract not only guys who want to get rich but guys who care how they win. We must provide an environment that results in the best products. Remember, Jerry Sanders is not the co-inventor of the microprocessor. They [staff] came to us because they thought we'd probably be a successful business. Engineers are like anyone else.

After a decade Sanders is as enthusiastic as ever and is dangling the presidency of AMD as a further incentive. In a brochure for prospective employees and others called "Put Yourself on the Line," he states:

> We're looking for a new president . . . [and] we promote from within. He or she will probably be an engineer. And . . . definitely . . . a striver, an achiever, an innovator. If you think you've got it, we'll give you the opportunity to go all the way—and kick me upstairs to chairman of the board.

Sanders will undoubtedly move to that position and stay there for many years. He is gaited for the long haul. As he comments: "I don't see any reason to change things just because I've made my bundle."

CAVEAT FOR SEMICONDUCTOR MAKERS: *Microprocessor price declines are to be expected, but 1980's jarring 60 percent slide—twice the norm—stunned the industry. Prices were still falling at press time due to twin factors of overcapacity and weaker demand reflecting high interest rates.*

AMD was hurt too. Its R&D outlays equal to 10 percent of sales contributed to flat profits in the March, 1981, quarter, but such spending is vital for technological leadership. Long-term holders hope for a return to 25 percent plus annual growth and big rewards several years out.

SUMMARY: *The pivotal microprocessor—the culmination of decades of computer development—was invented by Intel and raised to high-performance standards by Advanced Micro-Devices. In the new industrial revolution, everything springs from this basic invention.*

Investors who grasp the significance of the microprocessor and its ability to transform both computer and non-computer corporations into highly profitable vehicles are ready for the world of future stocks and the rich rewards investments in them will bring. Remember that most of the future stock rewards will come from companies that are not primarily semiconductor manufacturers.

4

Minicomputers and the Office of the Future

(Two High-Technology Turnarounds)

CONCEPT: *Some of the more mature minicomputer companies may no longer grow fast enough to make future stocks. But at least two minicomputer companies, both of which qualify as turnaround situations, may experience extraordinary growth and offer investors rich rewards as they move dramatically into new markets.*

Some background thoughts: In the 1960s, following the decade that established IBM as the dominant mainframe computer maker, a handful of smaller high-technology companies including Digital Equipment Corporation and Data General bravely raised their banners to do battle with the titan.

These companies developed new, smaller computers with considerable data processing capability. They then set their sights on some mainframe computer customers and on smaller sales prospects that had never before owned computers large or small.

Electronic Overkill

The minicomputer companies considered existing computer users to be a major potential market and persuaded some that costly mainframe computers were inappropriate for certain jobs—that their use in routine applications constituted the computer equivalent of employing a wine press to crack an egg, effective perhaps, but electronic overkill.

In these sales efforts the minicomputer makers often were abetted by computer programers who recommended minicomputers in efforts to land cost-conscious clients.

In the years that followed, thousands of minicomputer users delighted in modestly priced systems programed to facilitate many jobs previously assigned to mainframe machines. In a second sales thrust, the mini makers made pitches to many smaller businesses, convincing them that they too were ready for the computer age, that the minicomputer was an efficient, low-cost tool that could help reduce costs, for example, through the automation of payroll and accounting functions.

The minicomputer makers used state-of-the-art electronic parts to build their machines. But unlike IBM, a vertically integrated company manufacturing everything from semiconductors to typewriters, the mini makers were basically assemblers, skilled in circuitry design and assembly—especially so when the microprocessor, or "computer on a chip," was developed by Intel and Texas Instruments.

More vital to the minicomputer makers' success were their outstanding use of software and their low-cost products relative to the mainframe companies.

Explosive Growth in Mini-Power

In any case, the successful watched as their minicomputer sales exploded. Profits—and stock market gains—over the years have been gargantuan. But every business has its heyday. Already, there are those in Wall Street and in institutional investing circles who believe the golden era is over for most minicomputer makers. The skeptics believe it to be significant that Data General reported its first quarterly earnings decline in its eleventh year, namely, in the final period of the fiscal year ended September 29, 1979.

But did the lag in Data General earnings signal approaching market saturation for the minicomputer maker? It could be.

For investors, the fundamental question is whether Data General, still a relatively small company with sales of about $825 million, is approaching maturity as a business. Data General's most serious problem has been its copy-cat approach. It imitates Digital Equipment and should instead innovate on its own terms. For minicomputer purchasers constitute the single dynamic market for Data General—the company has 11 percent of that business—as the company is presently constituted. If the company were to use its strong base in minis to launch moves into highly profitable allied fields, Data General would be thrust into an underdog role. In fact, it must earn its gains of whatever dimension in minis for the foreseeable future. If the minicomputer market is nearing saturation, then Data General may well be past its peak.

High-Tech Marketing Strategy: Sidestep IBM

Huge though IBM is, it is not omnipresent. It cannot exploit every computer-related market. What Digital Equipment, Data General, and scores of others have done is to snatch the golden crumbs from IBM's table, exploiting dozens of lucrative billion-dollar markets. You'll find promising high-tech companies that are sidestepping IBM in the stock futures section and in the pages of the *Value Line Investment Survey* and other business reference works.

Digital Equipment Corporation: Junior IBM?

The question of maturity in the minicomputer market seems equally pertinent for Digital Equipment, a company often referred to as a junior IBM. Dynamic DEC anticipates that revenues will be close to $4 billion in the current fiscal year. Its great size suggests even more strongly that market saturation may be on the horizon. On the plus side, DEC has an overwhelming share of the minicomputer market in a business in which customer loyalty is dictated by the dual considerations of the need for equipment compatability and of obtaining service on equipment in place.

In contrast to DEC's 39 percent share, IBM has a mere 4 percent of the minicomputer market. Nobody can say whether the mini market is approaching saturation. Only time will tell. IBM itself grossly underestimated the market for mainframes years ago, predicting a leveling off at about the time the market was beginning to take off.

Try Soft Focus for a Clearer Picture

Distinctions between mainframes and minicomputers are blurring—particularly with the debut last year of the breadbox-sized mainframe on three chips. Thus, it is inappropriate to think of different-sized computers serving different markets. The question is whether a company is finding major new applications (that is, markets) regardless of the size or type of equipment it produces.

DEC officials optimistically predict that the company will continue to grow at a 30 percent annual rate through the 1980s. If so, that would make DEC one of the top industrial companies with $32 billion in sales by 1990. In comparison, IBM's sales in 1981 were less than $30 billion.

Even without adjustment for potential inflation, DEC's goal is awe-inspiring. Yet it could happen—especially now that DEC is expanding aggressively into distributed data processing and other burgeoning areas.

CAVEAT: *More than one analyst sees both Digital Equipment and Data General as unlikely to maintain traditional growth patterns—sees them as towering Himalayan peaks, but static, not unlike the Mount Everest that is IBM.*

The Office of the Future

There are fewer Cassandras among those watching Wang Laboratories and Datapoint and other computer companies that are exploiting the "office of the future" market. The office of the future, which is arriving with a rush, contemplates electronic links between computers, word processors, and other office equipment. Meantime, as we have already suggested, typewriters and filing cabinets will be downplayed, with records filed in electronic memories for ready reference and for updating via cathode ray tube display. The CRT screen is similar to the television screen and is linked to a keyboard for adding or deleting words and numbers to the data which are called up on the screen. In the office of the future, paper will be peripheral, not central. Minicomputer companies are well positioned to move into this multibillion dollar market. Wang Labs had seized the initiative more aggressively than either DEC or Data General.

Wang: Diehard Original

Wang was founded in 1951 by Dr. An Wang, a Harvard professor. Dr. Wang left the university to found a company that is older by several years than Digital Equipment. But Wang Labs developed by fits and starts as it explored various markets.

After a particularly dangerous exposure in the calculator business, a turnaround was fostered with two key new product lines unveiled in 1972—minicomputers and word processing systems. These efforts, shaky at first, ultimately became signally successful. Now in the dynamic word processing field, Wang is regarded as being second only to IBM. Thus, Wang is regarded as a comer—curiously enough, three decades after its founding.

Exciting New Avenues to Profits for Minimakers

Wang's story clearly suggests that makers and marketers of minicomputers must develop leadership positions in allied areas for continued success, areas like the office of the future where growth is unlikely to slow for years.

Just so, a revitalized Datapoint Corporation has marched with determination and effect to carve out a share of the office of the future market with its advanced dispersed data processing systems. Wall Streeters believe Wang and Datapoint will thrive as the office of the future develops.

An Wang: No Communist He

An Wang had just completed college at Chia Tung University in Shanghai in 1945. The fierce civil war that would bring the Chinese Communists to power was under way. Wang didn't stay for the ending. Luckily the Chiang government sent the promising young man to Harvard to learn about the blossoming science of electronics. Wang proved to be a superior student. He stayed to become a professor and eventually a capitalist. After inventing a core-memory system for computers, he founded his own company with a $500 investment. He called the company Wang Laboratories and chose Lowell, Massachusetts, as its headquarters. He has since amassed a fortune that would astound associates in China—and even those in the United States. Dr. Wang is worth several hundred million dollars.

Not that Dr. Wang followed a fast track to riches. There were years of mediocre results as Wang concentrated on customized, one-of-a-kind devices for the machine tool industry. It was a ho-hum business from Wall Street's point of view. But in 1964 a period of rapid growth began for Wang with the development of a line of engineering calculators. Between 1964 and 1972, revenues grew from a base of $1.6 million to a respectable $32 million.

But by then the calculator market was in turmoil, and things at Wang Labs were to get worse, much worse. As one critic comments: "Prior to and during the 1974–1975 recession, Wang tried to compete with Hewlett-Packard and IBM with an obsolescent desk calculator line and a poorly designed word processor product. The result was that while revenues grew by 325 percent between 1969 to 1975, earnings per share remained level in the range of 14 to 16 cents."

But An Wang wasn't finished. Unlike some other companies—including the now defunct builder of the Bowmar Brain—Wang recognized early that heavily capitalized competitors in the calculator market would threaten if not destroy those who remained in the arena. Thus he undertook his two-pronged developmental effort to design and perfect advanced data processing and word processing systems. Though the products didn't impress in the beginning, constant improvement

Minicomputers and the Office of the Future

eventually brought many fans. The two lines have since elevated the company to major success.

The Turnaround

What Wang did was marry word processing and data processing to form the basic tools for the office of the future. It is already clear that this market will be one of the hottest of the current decade, with optimists estimating sales of $30 billion by 1990.

Needless to say, the struggle for that market will be fierce. The list of companies competing for a share of the business reads like a roster of senior blue-chip high-tech companies. It starts with IBM and includes Xerox Corporation, and Honeywell, Inc. Even Exxon Corporation, through its technically advanced Vydec terminal and related information systems, is in the business.

But experts believe that Wang is outstanding in the fields of both computers and word processors, and that it takes expertise in each of these two areas to compete effectively. This assessment pleases An Wang immensely. "Other than IBM," he comments, "we're the only company that's strong on both sides."

Wang has modified both his minicomputers and his word processors to give each qualities possessed by the other. That is, he has added significant word processing capabilities to Wang's best "virtual storage" computers while building data processing capabilities into the Wang word processing office systems.

Outguessing the Pros: Most Won't Notice Return on Equity Is Soaring 'Til You've Made Your Bundle

Well-managed companies riding the success of great new inventions can experience rapidly rising returns on equity.

For example: Suppose return on equity capital is steady at 10 percent for four years and suddenly rises to 20 percent. Usually, it will be years after that before the stock goes up in adequate recognition of this extraordinary accomplishment.

Use Value Line's "% Earned Net Worth" figure as equiva-

> lent to return on common equity in measuring this factor. Meantime, note that important new inventions work especially well for smaller and medium-sized high-tech companies. They begin to experience economies of scale. That's why Wang, with revenues of under $200 million in the late 1970s, showed such extraordinary gains in return on equity and in the stock market following the introduction of its new systems.
>
> Incidentally, Wang was able to make telling inroads against competitors, including IBM, through judicious use of debt—particularly convertible debentures.

Thus either system allows customers to manipulate both words and data. Using a single terminal, then, a business user could, for example, compose the president's letter for an annual report and also perform calculations for the report's financial tables. New communications software is also available from Wang that will permit these systems to be linked together. This will make information instantly available everywhere within a business. Headquarters information will be called up on screens in field offices thousands of miles away, while field sales and inventory information will be available at the home office.

One system making all this possible is Wang's Mailway, which combines various company products to form an electronic network that can virtually eliminate the need for internal mail rooms and the need to place stamps on envelopes, put mail into bags for collection, and depend on the U.S. Post Office.

A "gateway" function allows Mailway users to send messages far beyond their own system, by linking to any private or commercial data network. That is, different users of Wang equipment can "mail" messages to each other directly. And Wang equipment can put messages into an addressee's non-Wang system through black box interconnectors.

In a related thrust, Wang is mating his word processing and computer systems to image printers and phototypesetting devices to create integrated information systems with the ability to publish without setting type.

It is already clear that the nation's office employees, including executives and secretaries, who are responsible for processing information and those who work with figures—bookkeepers, payroll, and accounting personnel among others—will be spending considerable time at computer terminals. The way it looks now, Wang will be a major supplier of the equipment to bring this about, and one of the toughest competitors. For Wang appears to have gone beyond basic hardware to adapt its terminals to serve the needs of the twenty-first-century office.

The Smartest Computer Companies Hold the Customer's Hand.

Baffled customers must be taught to understand the intricacies of their computer systems. For the carefully nurtured client is fiercely loyal—and a major source of repeat business. Thus, sums spent on sales—both direct and indirect—are among the most important.

While the era of the automated office is already here, many of the systems developed by major manufacturers baffle users. As Wang's vice president of marketing support, J. Carl Masi, comments, "IBM and Xerox design products, bring them to the customer and say, 'Take it or leave it.' We'll be more influenced by what customers want."

Easing the customer into the computer age is an old tradition at Wang. This is reflected again in the low-cost computers Wang introduced in 1977. These machines sported such advanced features as multiple interactive terminals, multilanguage, and simultaneous access to memory units and other peripherals. These features, advanced for their day, were enhanced by the use of the easy-to-learn BASIC programing language.

Masi comments: "Wang selected the popular BASIC programing language, used in over 30,000 of its small business computers, because it is the simplest language to learn and use, and because it provides the best bridge between number crunching and commercial data processing applications."

An analytical report by an institutional investor called The Boston Company elaborated on Wang's supportive approach, noting that the company's marketing program supports software vendors and assists customers who strive to develop their own software at reasonable costs. Vincent M. Cestari of The Boston Company stated recently:

> To be sure, this program is expensive [for Wang to install], as indicated by the 32.5 percent of revenues spent on selling and general administrative costs in a recent quarter, but it is effective because users perceive that they receive more support from Wang than from IBM.

Even so, the best high-tech companies that sell to the end user as Wang does generally spend over 30 percent for these items. As part of its unique marketing approach, Wang offers help to custom software houses in their efforts to write specialized programing for specific industries and then guides its own customers to these programs. While other manufacturers have developed this capability, they lag far behind Wang in office automation.

Test of Excellence: Sleeping Giant Wakes, Smaller Rival Still Outruns Him

Item: Suddenly aggressive IBM offered a fine new word processor in 1980 with one-year delivery. Four months later, Wang offered a better one for immediately delivery.

Wang's competitors can be expected to spend heavily to catch up in the years ahead, but Wang is likely to present a moving target. Its customer base is already formidable, and customer loyalty is helping Wang maintain its lead. Wang's existing customer base is said by Wang to produce 20 to 25 percent of the company's business.

What then are the risks at Wang? For one thing, Wang has an unusually high debt base for a high-technology company, though the company has been reducing its dependence on borrowings for some time. As recently as mid-1980, long-term debt was equal to 42 percent of capital against an industry average of 30 percent. But the company is replacing high-cost term loans and bank debt with the proceeds from a $100 million 25-year debenture issue sold in August of 1980.

Since the debentures are convertible into stock, Wang borrowed the funds at a 9 percent interest cost.

Wang Has Scored Heavily with Borrowed Capital

Wang's recent growth has been nothing short of phenomenal, with sales compounding at a 50 percent yearly rate and earnings rising equally rapidly. Result: Wang shares are up 30 times from the 1976 level—$10,000 invested then was worth well over $300,000 in 1980—and the company remains exceptionally well positioned for the 1980s.

Value Line thinks the potential dilution resulting out of conversion of the debenture will be minimal because of the stock's relatively high price-earnings ratio (discouragingly high for some investors at current levels, perhaps). The call for redemption of two earlier $50 million debenture issues added 10 percent more shares, but it raised equity per share by 37 percent.

Noting the company's relatively low research and development budget, equal to 7.7 percent of revenues, The Boston Company called this a tribute to the creativity of Dr. Wang. (High-tech companies commonly spend much more, with Data General at 10 percent, and DEC at 6.7 percent on its considerably larger base.) The Boston report continues:

> Dr. Wang through his own personal inventiveness has maintained an extremely high productivity level with an undersized R&D [effort]. It is obvious that without Dr. Wang (who is 60 years of age) the costs of R&D would be higher and the development pace would slow down.

Meanwhile, Dr. Wang's desire to improve products and to anticipate market developments can hurt. A good example of this was the unsuccessful introduction in 1978 of a fiber optics image printer, or intelligent copier.

Whatever happens, Wang will be a tough competitor for years in view of its pivotal position in the office of the future market. But IBM is no mean competitor, to mention just the foremost of Wang's many potential rivals in this vast new market. Whether it will be a future stock in the years ahead is not clear. But the situation is regarded as highly promising.

CAVEAT: *Wang has outgrown its maintenance and service capability and must greatly expand coverage here.*

On the Importance of Being Loyal to High-Tech Companies

Investors who grasp the role of customer loyalty in high-technology companies can make fortunes in these shares. There is a higher degree of loyalty here than in any other field.

Chivas Regal buyers aren't as brand loyal as people who buy computer systems.

Reason: Each producer's wares are unique. It is awkward for a customer, once a particular system is installed, to switch over to another. The cost of retraining people and reprograming may be prohibitive.

(Those stuck with marginal systems become resigned, taking the attitude of Americans who years ago propped up an unpopular regime in Asia. Someone said that the Asian president was a son of a bitch. A top American official responded wearily, "Yes, but he's OUR son of a bitch.")

Generally, it is a bad idea for investors to get involved in a high-tech company in which loyalty is not important.

Eventually, competition will maim or even kill the company. The Bowmar (Brain) Calculator Company is a good example. There was no reason for loyalty there. When the competition galvanized into action and the price of calculators came down, customers bought superior models from Bowmar's rivals.

Investors have suffered spectacular losses in high-tech shares due to a failure to evaluate the loyalty factor. Losing sight of the importance of this factor may be the single biggest mistake an investor in high-tech shares can make.

Datapoint: Another Classic Turnaround

With the bold words, "It's Datapoint's long-range goal to automate everything that can be automated in a typical business office," the company's resident master of research and development, Senior Vice President Victor D. Poor, tells what role he expects for Datapoint in the office-of-the-future market. The statement would have brought hollow laughter just half a dozen years ago, when Datapoint was fighting for survival.

Datapoint was a perfect example of an exciting innovator jeopardized by a lack of strong management, the sine qua non of any successful business.

Founded as Computer Terminal Corporation in mid-1968 during the peak of a great bull market, the company was soon mired in deficits. By 1972, when stock market and business conditions generally were grim, the situation was even worse at the fledgling computer products company. Were it not for the arrival of a new top-management team led by Harold E. O'Kelley, an experienced high-tech manager who joined as president and chairman in 1973, the company probably would be defunct today.

One of the first things the new management did was to rename the company Datapoint to identify it more closely with the product line. That product line is "dispersed data processing systems," to use the generic terminology. The small Datapoint processors are actually fully compatible small computer systems. These systems allow the sharing of common data bases and provide data processing at decentralized locations throughout the organization—where data originates and where much of the results of the data processing are needed.

One of Datapoint's seminal products—Attached Resource Computer Software Architecture—allows an arbitrary number of Datapoint processors, linked together by communication lines, to function as a single integrated computer facility and to share a common base of data. Meantime, each individual processor or terminal can perform tasks on a stand-alone basis as well.

Stephen T. McClellan, a financial analyst at Salomon Brothers, comments that

> This [stand-alone] facility is an increasingly integral part of the overall system and enables Datapoint processors and peripherals to carry out many functions. . . . The only feature that ever needs [changing is] the software. . . . The incremental cost to customers in adding new software is considerably less than adding dedicated, stand-alone pieces of computer hardware, as would be required for most of Datapoint's competitors.

Thus, a Datapoint ARC user can add the exact amount of processing or storage capacity whenever and wherever it is needed on a modular basis. Critical to Datapoint's success: Elements of the system are cheap enough to be purchased through normal channels and without approval of top management. According to Datapoint, "The customer buys them like typewriters, copiers, or any other piece of equipment needed to run the day-to-day business."

Like the more costly systems of competitors, Datapoint's systems can be used in a wide variety of applications, including business data processing, communications, word processing, and electronic mail. To emphasize: Every office worker with an ARC processor or terminal has direct access to the full range of computer power and stored data. But, add-on capability distinguishes Datapoint from larger computer systems for distributed data processing such as those offered by Wang Laboratories. While there is some competition between Datapoint and Wang and others offering larger systems such as Hewlett-Packard and IBM, Wang, et al., are busy creating new markets or catering to existing customer bases.

The Drones and the Queen Bees

The important difference between distributed data processing and processing by mainframe computer is that distributed data processing terminals are not "drones" but intelligent "queen bees" as it were—minimainframes with their own data banks and processing capability. Further, distributed data sys-

> tems offer each user immediate access to data stored in the individual terminals.
>
> By contrast, mainframe computer systems use drone terminals and centralize data storage and processing in the mainframe—à la Wang, et al. Mainframe systems usually offer limited access—a set number of terminals can be employed at a time. On the other hand, more queen bee terminals can be added to distributed data processing systems as needed. Many regard Datapoint's low-cost system as a standout in the field.

Datapoint and other similar systems pose a dilemma for IBM, which is becoming a more aggressive factor in this market. IBM must proceed cautiously or suffer an undesirable impact on its own revenue base. That is, the heart of IBM's business is still computer mainframes. To the extent that distributed data processing moves computer processing power from the central site to smaller processors, the adoption of distributed processing reduces mainframe requirements.

But just how rosy is the future for Datapoint? That company and its chief rival, Four-Phase, each hold major market shares while Digital Equipment, Raytheon, Pertec, Univac, IBM, Mohawk, Sycor, and Nixdorf each hold a share of the remaining market.

What makes Datapoint the company to beat in Wall Street's view is its management. Of the top four men, only research director Poor was at the firm when Mr. O'Kelley arrived in 1973. Mr. O'Kelley brought with him from Harris Corp. Richard V. Palermo, executive vice president for operations—Mr. O'Kelley's heir apparent—and E. Gistaro, executive vice president for corporate development.

Harris has supplied managers to others all too frequently, from its point of view. As Salomon's McClelland notes, most of Datapoint's top management have large-company backgrounds, with Mr. Palermo and Mr. O'Kelley having academic experience as well. Before joining Harris, Mr. Gistaro was with Honeywell and RCA, while Mr. Palermo was with IBM. The age spread within top management ranges from the upper thirties to the mid-fifties. McClelland writes: "Since Datapoint is small and growing rapidly, promotions are rapid and upward mobility is substantial. Most promotions have been from within."

Evidently management has impressed the work force with its fairness and its desire to please. There are no labor unions.

Management skills are broad, including those of engineering, marketing, and research and development. Financial backgrounds are notably absent, Mr. McClelland says, except in the case of the vice president for finance, ". . . Yet the company has excellent financial characteristics."

The Salomon analyst referred in part to the fact that shortly after the new management was installed, debt was virtually eliminated through conversion into common shares.

A high-tech company such as Datapoint thrives on its ability to keep ahead of the pack. Thus it should be noted that research and development are emphasized at the top-management level. In the fiscal 1979 proxy statement, two of the five members of upper management listed were in R&D.

Revenues have soared to over $300 million and appear likely to grow at a 25 percent or better rate in the years immediately ahead, while profits have grown at an impressive 40 percent rate compounded over the past five years. Some believe profits will grow at a rate of well over 25 percent annually for years to come.

Does this mean that Datapoint is decidedly a future stock? It is hard to say.

CAVEAT: *Datapoint faces contingencies that could hurt this fine company. For one thing, there is potential competition from the world's largest industrial company, American Telephone.*

Even so, the shares have been popular with institutional holders, and the future seems bright. Datapoint, in any event, resembles Wang to a degree. Both are classic examples of well-executed high-technology turnarounds—something that can make lots of money for alert investors in high-technology stocks.

Overlooked Opportunity

Keep in mind that many investors do not fully understand how distributed data processing works and have thus neglected this major area of growth in computer science.

SUMMARY: *Mainframe or mini? It is important to think in terms of the market a computer company serves rather than whether that company builds mainframes or minicomputers.*

This is clear from the fact that minicomputer makers Wang and Datapoint have risen from the ashes to become leaders in major markets against mainframe builder IBM. Wang did it through superior product and by lavishing tender loving care on its minicomputer customers, and Datapoint by circumscribing the need for mainframes through batteries of "intelligent" terminals that store, share, and process data.

5

Service for Supergrowth

CONCEPT: *The best computer services companies are flexible enough to grow rapidly. Those who believe cheap computing power threatens this billion-dollar industry are wrong.*

First some background. Software is the connective tissue that makes computers work. Without it, mainframe units are merely expensive hardware with little utility, and microprocessors just so much idle refined sand. There are a number of computer services companies that use software in ways basic to their businesses—though they may do so by performing quite different functions. Some, like Automatic Data Processing, design software for their own computers that has general application. Thus, ADP offers computerized payroll preparation services to thousands of businesses. Others, like Cullinane, design software for sale to the business community for use by in-house computer personnel. Many believe there is dazzling potential in both areas.

The Old Piano Roll Blues

There has been speculation that the era of computer software—by analogy, the paper music roll for the player piano—will end before it fully blossoms. Specifically, some believe computer hardware under development will be so powerful that it won't be necessary to design elegant computer software. Problems will be solved through "brute force," as the computer experts say.

To follow the player piano example: Consider the child who attempts to pick out familiar tunes on the piano. Nothing elegant about this trial-and-error method. Nevertheless, assuming the child can make tonal distinctions, the melody may emerge, however raggedy.

A powerful computer that is programed in a rudimentary manner can also solve simple problems by trial-and-error methods and with commendable speed. All we see is the end results: Unlike the cacaphonous errors of the hunt and peck pianist, computer mistakes are unseen and unheard—mute miscues in microscopic circuits. The argument for this electronic approach is, "Who cares if the method is inefficient so long as it is accomplished as rapidly as required?"

For a practical example of the brute-force approach, give a computer a lengthy list of names and instruct it to alphabetize them. If the computer must rely on standardized instructions for frequently used procedures rather than software tailored to do the job, an electronic hunt and peck will ensue; considerable time will elapse before the list is ready—unless, of course, a very powerful computer is used.

Brute Force or Electronic Judo?

Why brute force? The argument is that if there is sufficient computer power available so that jobs can be done with brute force, a shortage of computer programers now reaching alarming proportions may be eliminated.

The hope has been that superchips would evolve with many times the power of older chips and that programing could be standardized for many functions, thus freeing programers for more rewarding tasks.

It is the central thesis of this book that high technology is moving ahead with impressive speed. Here's proof: While this book was in preparation, new devices have been developed that standardize many programing functions. While a number of companies have worked on this sort of equipment, Intel has stolen the march with the most promising offering—a micromainframe—to date.

Intel's new micromainframe includes an imbedded operating system that does in fact simplify programing. Tests indicate Intel's micromainframe-on-three-chips will increase programer productivity by 800 percent.

Here's an example of what this will mean.

Assume it takes a computer 10 hours to perform a certain complex function using standard procedures. Assume further that a programer working 100 hours can create a software program that can reduce elapsed time on the computer to one hour. If that program is to be employed again and again, it makes sense to order the software.

But if new microcomputers can do the job in one hour through brute force, their cheap power—though employed without the elegance of superior programing—will suffice to do the job. This would have to be done at a cost that is competitive with that incurred when a programer is employed to solve the problem with elegant software on a less-advanced computer. Intel is making this happen.

This has caused some unsophisticated investors to assume that computer services companies generally will become obsolete—whether they serve client corporations by custom designing software for in-house use, or employ software directly in providing clients with payroll services and the like on a contract basis.

But it doesn't work that way. Remember that those who pump the pedals on the player piano rarely learn to play the instrument. The player roll may be produced more rapidly and may play more difficult pieces, but it is as essential as ever. Without it, the instrument is mute in the hands (or feet) of the user.

The service companies won't be hurt. Instead it will be easier—and cheaper—for the software companies to produce their wares. Most customers would like a lot more data processing, but there are so few programers that backlogs exist for several years' worth of computer services.

The software companies are not even threatened by the Japanese, who have aimed their important competitive thrusts at the hardware makers. In software applications, the United States leads the world and by a substantial margin.

Survival of the Fittest

Just how real is the threat to the computer services companies? Mark Twain, as we all know, responded to some premature obituaries published about himself with the words, "Reports of my death are greatly exaggerated." Computer services companies can relate to that. These corporations may not have as good a shot at immortality as Twain did, but to hear them tell it, their chances of survival are far greater than any mortal's.

Self-conscious the computer services companies most certainly are. Lightly capitalized by industrial standards and with little if any manufacturing muscle, some argue that they are as essential as a spare ship captain. Sure, the supercargo captain can "pilot" the computers, but once computers become more sophisticated, once they can respond, for example, to instructions written in Americanese, who needs outsiders? Those who take a dim view of the computer services industry's future insist that once it is possible for unskilled employees to run the computers, the service company will cease to exist.

The industry confronted this prospect at the First World Computing Services Industry Congress in Barcelona in 1978, asking itself rhetorically a number of fundamental questions. Was computer service really an industry or just a coincidence? Did ". . . circumstances permit [it] to develop when the need for better information was not being met by the tools available?"

Investors who own shares in computer services companies will be reassured to know that the industry resolves these and other fundamental questions in its own favor. Back in 1978 it was argued at the conference that computer service was not "simply a bridge from the early days of expensive computer resources to the cheap new technology which will reclaim the customers we so faithfully served for three decades."

May We Hear from a Pioneer, Please?

Frank R. Lautenberg, chairman of the board of Automatic Data Processing, addressed these concerns at that Barcelona conference. It was as good a place as any to hold a survival conference. The venerable city was created by third-century Phoenicians.

Mr. Lautenberg said skeptics would argue that computer services companies have merely "penetrated the soft spots in the monolith of hardware-oriented, in-house data processing." He went on to argue:

> Hopefully, without being too harsh, we might characterize such people as "technologically oriented," firm in their belief that for every information problem facing businessmen there is a hardware solution.
>
> They see each press announcement of a new processor, faster memory, or cheaper disk drives as another nail in the services' coffin.

But the appeal of that argument, he said, is "simplistic."

> What such [critics of the service industry] fail to recognize is the natural adaptability, the resilience, and the resourcefulness that this industry has developed over a lengthy period of time.

He drew an analogy to the advent of television and what that had meant to radio and later to the movies. Radio was in limbo for a while, but there are now five times as many radio stations as there were in the 1940s when commercial TV was born. Then in 1950 television began to worry film producers, as people shunned the movie houses and sat around the home theater as television developed its own dramatized stories. TV's golden era of great drama came early in the game. But the movie companies survived too and today are doing exceptionally well.

His conclusion was that the computer services companies will survive and thrive—grandly, not ignominiously.

The key point: The advantage enjoyed by the computer services companies is in their specialized knowledge. They are extremely stable companies because clients cannot duplicate the service companys' expertise on their own.

Let's Talk Automatic Data Processing, Inc.

Mr. Lautenberg then sketched the history of his company, a pioneer in computer services, and he did so in a way that raises the curtain for those who find most things associated with computers arcane and difficult to relate to. The early history of his company shows how basic the work is that computers have undertaken.

First Mr. Lautenberg called attention to the size of his giant company. At present, ADP, Inc., employs 12,700 people. That figure was 9,000 three years ago when he spoke in Barcelona. ADP now has over 70,000 payroll accounts. ADP has half a hundred computer centers throughout the world and operates nearly 400 computer systems, ranging from Digital Equipment Corp.'s small PDP-8 minicomputer units through a full range of major manufacturers' equipment, including the giant Amdahl 470-V6.

Revenues broke through the half-billion-dollar level in the 12 months ended December, 1980—up from $300 million at the time of the speech.

Among the company's proudest boasts: 77 consecutive quarters of year-to-year growth in excess of 15 percent in both revenue and earnings.

The interesting part of the story, the part that makes the company's *raison d'être* clear to all, is ADP's origins.

Putting Payroll in Perspective

A little more than 30 years ago, Henry Taub was a twenty-one-year-old accountant. He had noticed that payrolls caused constant problems for smaller companies. While payrolls were relatively easy to do, a simple clerical function, highly skilled people inevitably were involved—accountants, office managers, and even senior executives.

Two major factors caused this imbalance of function and skill. The first was time demand. Payroll schedules had to be met regardless of any other business requirements, and the payrolls had to be absolutely accurate. "Each employee was an expert auditor when it came to his own paycheck," as Mr. Lautenberg points out. Second, the information was sensitive. Employers demanded confidentiality to avoid trouble resulting from employee disputes over wages.

Timeliness and secrecy combined to create a situation where the cost of preparation far exceeds the value of the skills necessary. Henry Taub sensed a real opportunity. He created ADP for the express purpose of doing company payrolls at realistic cost.

Here were the economics in 1949: The job could have been handled by a clerk at a $40 a week wage. But senior bookkeepers making not less than $80 to $100 a week invariably became involved, too. And that direct expense wasn't the whole story. Time was diverted to payroll that could be spent more productively. Because of the demands of payroll, order processing, the collecting of outstanding accounts, and the discounting of vendor bills—not to mention numerous other more important activities—were neglected.

In 1949 it took an average of two days a week to process a 100-person payroll. Thus these relatively small companies gave over 100 days of management attention per year to a low-order clerical function.

So ADP (then Automatic Payrolls, Inc.) began providing an alternative. Raw payroll data was picked up from the client, taken to the company's processing center, and returned with checks ready for signature. The cost in those early days was $25 for a 100-employee payroll.

The Better Mouse Trap May Be a Hard Sell

Surprisingly though, the service was a hard sell. The information was so sensitive that management didn't want to pass it to an outsider. What's more, prospective customers wondered whether the fledgling service company would survive to complete the annual cycle for tax returns and year-end closing.

Arrangements between ADP and clients were somewhat tentative as a result. Mr. Lautenberg said, "There were no contracts between our payroll clients and us—just as there are none today. Performance was measured on a week-to-week basis by the customer, and the relationship stood or fell based on that performance."

The equipment was primitive by today's standards: a mechanical

Service for Supergrowth   93

bookkeeping machine to post amounts on checks and indicate deductions from gross wages to arrive at take-home pay. Some peripherals included an Addressograph machine using metal plates to print names, some Friden calculators, and a few ancient Victor Comptometers. "The most important tool of the trade then was the sharpened pencil and the skill of its user."

In the beginning things were rough—the prospects unclear, and aspirations modest, as they so frequently are in a startup situation. The idea was clearly more valuable than anyone realized, even the employees. Mr. Lautenberg joined the company as a part-timer in 1952. He recalled:

> I had faith in the concept, but insufficient conviction to put my career on the line with a company doing $35,000 a year in revenues. Certainly we could not envision the ultimate opportunity. Our focus was on the obligation to turn out the almost-perfect product on a most unreasonable time schedule for a very modest fee. Henry [Taub] and I only aspired to "earn a living" one day from payroll service. If someone had suggested a $10 million company, it would have seemed as absurd as the idea that some day man would walk on the moon.

An Important Aside

It is worth noting here that often people are either too optimistic or too pessimistic about the prospects of an infant company. Gaining a perspective is never easy, but those who are able to analyze prospects realistically and at an early point in the game are most likely to earn profits in future stocks. Fortunately, the biggest rewards for investors usually come in companies that go public after a market for their products has been established and the future is reasonably clear—Genentech to the contrary notwithstanding.

Growing Up with ADP

In his Barcelona speech, Mr. Lautenberg made some comments about the business that may help investors avoid glamour for glamour's sake. The comments suggest technology's limits as well as its potential.

While computers were under intensive development in ADP's early days, the company felt no compulsion to get involved early. Lautenberg said:

> Our customers were not concerned with the means we used to provide a solution to their payroll problems. We were never asked whether we were using the newest accounting machine or a dated version, whether delivery would be made by bus, truck, or car, or where we saw the future. No one cared how fancy our offices were. We rarely, if ever, had a visitor. The only thing we could offer was the reputation derived from a few satisfied customers when the going was, indeed, very tough.
>
> The customer's only concern, as it is today, was our ability to deliver the promised service. The methods we chose for the preparation of the paycheck were selected based on the minimum needed to get the job done properly.
>
> In those early days we established a principle: We would never be swept off our feet by the most technologically advanced or elegant systems.

Enter Computers, Slowly

> In fact, ADP did not computerize until 1961, when we brought in our first IBM 1401. To emphasize the obvious, that was 12 years after the founding of the company, and I remember very clearly the revenues for that year reached $400,000. The pace could not have been slower; the education more thorough, nor the foundation better prepared for the opportunities and changes that were ahead.
>
> The simple principles were firmly established: a basic service for which there is a widespread need, a determination to deliver a quality product, and a steadfast refusal to be enchanted with what in the old days would have been called "bells and whistles."

The company went public in 1961, the year it bought that IBM 1401, and was soon a speculative favorite at an amazing and undoubtedly unjustified 90 times earnings. But ADP was soundly managed. The top executives resisted the temptation to use the stock as "Chinese

Service for Supergrowth

paper" to become a conglomerate—by moving into areas it didn't understand. ADP executives always asked themselves, "What would happen if the experts acquired in an acquisition decided to do something else?"

Wise. This single-purpose computer services company has thrived through acquisitions of companies very like itself, while the conglomerates of the era that haven't actually gone bankrupt have been disappointments, by and large.

As Mr. Lautenberg points out, anyone who gambled on ADP with a 100-share purchase of the company's initially offered shares in 1961 paid $3 a share—$300. Today, as a result of splits, those shares would number 3,600, valued at more than $100,000 as this book went to press. Annual dividends at the current rate would total $1,684 on those shares. A $10,000 investment in 1961 would be worth $3,300,000 today.

ADP now offers dozens of computer services to a vast variety of companies and it is a fixture in the world of business, as are many other companies in this $6 billion segment of the computer industry.

> CAVEAT: *ADP is offered primarily for illustrative purposes in that its story explains what service companies are all about. In future, ADP, large and relatively slow-moving, will be hard-pressed to meet the 26 percent annual growth standards expected of future stocks, impressive though its traditional 15 percent rate of growth is. Significantly, ADP shares have gained little ground in the past ten years.*
>
> *ADP sells an unexciting product—expertise and reliability. While other, smaller companies offering similar services may qualify as future stocks, ADP does not. Moreover, it is primarily the computer services companies offering software that have remarkable growth prospects.*
>
> *Top software companies are hard to beat as future stock candidates. Few are threatened by the Japanese. In software applications, Uncle Sam is king.*

To the Industry, Then

As Mr. Lautenberg said of the computer services industry generally, "The success of our companies rests now, as it did [a generation ago], on how well we satisfy the customer, rather than how satisfied we are with our technological achievements."

Are these businesses, then, unusually profitable? And will the best companies earn enough to qualify them for our select list of future stocks? It would appear so.

Mr. Lautenberg noted in his speech that revenues for a group of ten publicly traded independent United States based computer services companies had grown at an average of 26 percent a year for the five years leading up to 1978.

Even more impressive, after-tax profits for the same ten companies increased at a rate of 37 percent a year during that same period. Mr. Lautenberg contrasted these results with the revenue and after-tax profit gains of the six largest mainframe computer markers themselves—up only 13 and 15 percent, respectively.

Opening the Passages of the Corporate Memory

The movie *Three Faces of Eve* portrayed the difficulties faced by a woman and her family as they grappled with her three distinct personalities. But the woman upon whose life the film was based was an unfortunate with several additional selves. The filmmakers dropped the remaining personalities so that a complex story could be told simply enough for moviegoers to follow.

Imagine a corporation with a dozen separately functioning personalities. Crazy? It certainly is. But this has happened throughout industry as over the years businesses have added a variety of imperfect computer systems to serve disparate corporate needs.

To wit, personnel has considerable information in a computer memory bank that would be useful to payroll and vice versa. But normally there is little if any sharing of the data base nor do changes made in the data in one system necessarily go to others with a com-

Service for Supergrowth

mon need for that data. Here's a simple example of the kind of thing that happens. An employee submits a change of address to payroll only to discover later that the personnel department, the credit union, and three or four other departments are still sending mail to the prior residence.

Naturally, the corporation's various data banks contain much redundant information as well as much data that is not replicated where needed. For example, a major company like General Motors may have data bases at scores of separate plants. If nonsensitive information in the various memory banks were available to computer terminal operators throughout the business—just as all the information in a healthy non-schizophrenic's memory is available when needed—the corporation would function better. Still, data base A cannot invade data base B, however routine the sought-after information may be. The various banks constitute discrete data crannies.

Even when one computer system can copy from another within the corporation, there will be problems. Alfred Berkeley, a computer software analyst from the Baltimore-based brokerage house, Alex. Brown & Co., explained with the following example.

Name, Rank, and Serial Number, Please

Suppose one data bank has name, rank, and social security number for each employee. Suppose a terminal on that system wants identical information on a number of employees at a plant on another system. That's fine, if the information is listed in the manner required. But suppose the plant at which the second system is found records employee age and sex as well—to meet Federal requirements, for example. Said Mr. Berkeley:

> The way computers are utilized, the operator would tap instructions on his terminal to "open personnel file and get name, rank, and social security number"—a, b, and c data on specific employees. But if the plant system has added age and sex—d and e items—the terminal on the first system would receive a, b, and c data for the first employee, and the first employee's d and e data for the information requested on the second em-

ployee, along with the appropriate *a* item for the second employee. Obviously, things would deteriorate rapidly thereafter. The printout would be garbage.

As a result of these problems—never completely solved, by the way—60 percent of programing time has been spent on so-called maintenance of old programs, keeping the various corporate computer systems up to date. Thus, in most corporations, only 40 percent of the corporation programmers' time has been available for writing new programs. The 60 percent devoted to maintenance did nothing new or productive, it simply solved the old problems all over again.

Enter Data Base Management

What the corporate world has needed is data base management. Computer services companies have sprung up to supply this need. What a data base management system does is to keep only one file with specific information and provide access to that file from any terminal.

Thus, regardless of which computer user taps out a request for information, the response will come and it will come from the only data base containing that information, regardless of where that data is in the organization. This assumes, of course, that the information the terminal user is seeking is not embargoed. That is, payroll data would not pop up on a terminal screen unless the user had a computer password entitling him to dip into that part of the data bank.

Cullinane Database Systems to the Rescue

One company has worked so intensively in this area that it has recently changed its name from Cullinane Corporation to Cullinane Database Systems. What Cullinane has done is to "write"— program—a data base management system that has broad application. The system is flexible enough for use in both profit and nonprofit corporations, in military organizations, and in a wide variety of government applications, all without significant modification.

Cullinane is not an Automatic Data Processing, Inc. Technically

Service for Supergrowth

speaking, ADP is a "batch" processor that receives a "batch" of payroll records from the customer, processes them, and returns employee checks written on the client's account for corporate signature.

Cullinane does not participate in any client's day-to-day corporate affairs. Instead, it sells to its computer-using clients its data base management program. The client's own programers save significant amounts of time since they do little programing maintenance and do not write redundancy into the various data banks.

To repeat, for the individual at the computer terminal, Cullinane and other data base management systems companies make it possible to obtain information wherever it may be in the corporate system by simple, direct command.

Cullinane's competitors include IBM, the largest factor in the market, private companies, Mathematica, whose shares are traded over the counter, and Applied Data Research, an American Stock Exchange company.

While all bear watching, Cullinane, an over-the-counter company, is bigger than its competitors relative to IBM yet small enough to appeal to investors seeking companies in an early stage of growth. Even so, Cullinane has its work cut out for it.

Why Cullinane?

Here are some comments from brokerage houses: Oppenheimer & Co., Inc., began following Cullinane late in 1980, saying:

> We have added Cullinane ... the largest and fastest-growing independent vendor of data base management software packages, to our coverage of the computer software and services industry. Despite the small size—revenues of $20 million for the fiscal year ... ended [April, 1980] —Cullinane has managed to compete successfully against IBM in the $140 million market for IBM-compatible data base management software.

Echoing these sentiments, Eberstadt said it believed that Cullinane should continue to benefit from its "solid reputation" in the data base management field. "Management's ability to purchase outside software packages/licenses and integrate them with its existing product line should also be of value." The shares were recommended for their long-term prospects.

Whatever happens to Cullinane, the field of data base management is an important one and could lead to major profits for investors who ferret out the companies with the best prospects.

Note: Cullinane is growing faster than before as the programer pinch worsens.

Growth of computer software companies generally is accelerating as the shortage of programers forces more and more corporations to seek outside assistance to meet their data processing needs.

CAVEAT: *While Cullinane has been exceptionally successful so far, IBM offers and will continue to offer stiff competition. This is not one of the areas IBM has neglected, but one heavily backed by its powerful marketing organization.*

Shared Medical Systems Cures Hospital Ills

Shared Medical Systems was founded in 1969 in the wake of President Johnson's Great Society legislation that established a major role for government in medical care services in this nation. As so frequently happens in high technology, Shared Medical represented a venture by renegades from a major high-technology company who sensed an opportunity that their employer either did not sense or else chose not to exploit. Former employees of IBM set up Shared Medical as a computer service company. R. James Macaleer, president and chairman of the company, explains:

> Shared Medical Systems provides information processing services for health care organizations (primarily acute-care hospitals). The types of financial and administrative services that we offer include . . . bed management, patient billing, third-party and insurance billing, statistical reporting, general ledger and financial reporting, inventory, and fixed asset accounting.

Service for Supergrowth

We also process patient medical data. We offer medical records indexing, patient care level analysis to determine (appropriate) staffing levels, clinical laboratory reporting, medication ordering and patient medication profiles, and utilization review reporting, both concurrent and retrospective.

In this day of government payments for hospital care, utilization review is essential. The hospital must determine that the patient's admission was necessary and that his stay does not continue for too long or he may not be eligible for insurance coverage involving government funds—Medicare and Medicaid.

The Network Approach

Shared Medical Systems receives its data via a communications network between company headquarters and the 475-plus hospitals it serves. Mr. Macaleer continued:

Each hospital has one or more terminals which are connected to our single data processing center in suburban Philadelphia by means of leased telephone wires.

Each hospital enters its data into our system through its terminal. At the data center the information is processed, stored, and used to prepare reports. These reports are printed on the hospital's terminal, or, if a report is too voluminous, it is printed at our data center on paper or microfiche and shipped to the hospital.

The company also installs minicomputers in hospitals. Half of Shared Medical System's client hospitals have minicomputers and use them for local processing of specialized programs. Meanwhile Shared Medical spends heavily on product development—8 percent of sales, which totaled over $100 million in 1980.

While many kinds of companies that serve the infirm are expected to suffer as government demands more and more efficiency, Shared Medical Systems, in the eyes of some Wall Street houses, will not be one of them. Rather, the perception is that Shared Medical Systems may well benefit as hospitals scramble to meet tougher standards, seeking computer assistance for tasks that are handled inefficiently at present.

Conceivably, Shared Medical's earnings may benefit as a result of a gradually aging population and a sharp increase in the total number of physicians—assuming that the competition doesn't catch up. IBM offers competition of a different sort. Shared Medical's three founders, Mr. Macaleer, Harvey J. Wilson, and Clyde Hyde, formerly were marketing representatives engaged in selling IBM's in-house computer systems to hospitals.

It is believed that a continuing trend toward specialized medical and surgical practices should also benefit Shared Medical because of a proliferation of tests, procedures, and equipment required by these new medical and surgical practices.

From Smaller to Larger Hospitals?

So far, Shared Medical has found a market among small and medium-sized hospitals, but as services have broadened, large hospitals with more than 500 beds may be prospects.

Dennis Q. Sherve, who follows Shared Medical for Morgan Stanley, wrote that most big hospitals use in-house computers, so this market is relatively untapped by outside service vendors and represents a substantial opportunity to earn larger revenues than most current hospital clients produce. Mr. Sherve says:

> We estimate (that) Shared Medical Systems currently serves 132,000 beds, or 15 percent of the short-term acute-care hospital beds in the United States. With its constantly improving system, we believe the company can increase its domestic market penetration by 1 percent to 2 percent per year for the foreseeable future.

Like other computer software producers that process at a central location, Shared Medical Systems has an edge. As John M. Nehra of Alex Brown, the Baltimore brokerage house, explains, the company understands the financial and operating requirements of hospitals and this is reflected in its data processing. As a result, the company's operating expenses have been reduced to a point at which Shared Medical Systems appears to Mr. Nehra to be one of the most efficient computer services companies.

What Multiple?

Does the company deserve a premium price-earnings multiple of 20 or more—which it usually gets? Obviously, there are those who believe it does. As one observer comments: "The balance sheet is in good shape. Internal cash flow has always been healthy, and most of Shared Medical's computer hardware is leased. That's why funded debt accounts for less than 20 percent of total capital."

Does this mean that Shared Medical is a future stock? It was in the past. Those who held stock in mid-1977 would have been worth five times as much by the end of 1980. That is, a $10,000 investment would have been worth $50,000. The business, relatively small even now, could grow by leaps and bounds if the company proves able to add significantly to billings of present customers and is also able to crack the big hospital market.

CAVEAT: *Shared Medical System's remarkable rate of growth could slow if the market for its hospital services turns out to be more limited than its boosters believe it to be.*

In any case, the three companies reviewed here—Automatic Data Processing, Cullinane, and Shared Medical—are classic examples of the way good computer service companies succeed, whether they are batch processors or suppliers of sophisticated software. You, the investor, should measure other portfolio candidates against the techniques developed by these successful companies.

SUMMARY: *A number of computer services companies will grow with unusual rapidity in the years ahead—partly as a result of the shrinking supply of computer programmers relative to the needs of a burgeoning market place.*

Generally speaking, software constitutes a bigger idea than service. Ergo, more software companies are likely to become future stocks than service companies.

Keep this thought in mind: In an era of super-high inflation, shares of software companies make superior holdings because the software companies don't need much new investment for added growth. In effect, they capitalize on prior research and development expenditures. So what if programers' salaries go up fast? So do the prices of old, standard programs which they continue to sell.

Incidentally, CAD/CAM companies are basically software companies—as we shall see.

6

CAD/CAM Does It Best

CONCEPT: *One key to our industrial regeneration in an increasingly competitive world is enhanced productivity resulting out of CAD/CAM. The august National Science Foundation's Center for Productivity says, "Computer-aided design and manufacturing equipment . . . has more potential to radically increase productivity than any development since electricity." Obviously, there may be future stocks among CAD/CAM companies—and, perhaps, in seemingly prosaic machine tool manufacturers, too.*

Scenario: Modern Times Revisited

The factory is unmanned and looks abandoned. Yet it operates at full tilt. It is as though the workers had left hastily for a fire drill and neglected to close down. But there is no sign of chaos, there are no finished parts spinning senselessly in the lathes. Rather, mechanical fingers methodically move unprocessed parts into milling machines at cadenced intervals. Later, the parts are shifted to the next station, until another step in the manufacturing process is completed. Clearly there is no disorder here. Quite the contrary. The machines mill and whir, grind and revolve through the day and into the night—sometimes for 24 hours without a pause—as though controlled by an unseen presence. And controlled they are. Supervisors sit in nearby soundproof rooms watching television monitors to make sure nothing slips out of kilter to damage parts. (Everyone has opened a book with pages that didn't get cut at the bottom; this is because the cutter gets out of adjustment. Similar things happen in factories as vibration causes setscrews and other mechanical parts to move slightly out of true.)

Actually, the plants could be overseen from home, but supervisors demanded their privacy and derailed that penny-saving scheme. Small matter. The automated factory is so trouble-free that down-time for adjustment and repair—a bugaboo that can nip 40 percent from production time in manned plants—is less than 10 percent.

At present, there are just a few of these plants in the entire world, yet they represent the future—the automated factory where unmanned machining centers turn out parts, around the clock, unattended, under the guidance of the manufacturer's computerized numerical control.

Look Ma, No Pencil!

That's the manufacturing side. Graphically the future has arrived more quickly. With computer-aided design equipment, one skilled designer-draftsman can accomplish in hours what used to take days. Error-free, concise computer-based drawings can be made from designs sketched on a cathode ray tube screen (similar to a television screen) by a designer who has been relieved of the tedium of actually drawing by thousands of software aids. His stylus is a magic wand that instantly calls from the computer memory bank straight lines, curves, and circles in whatever size he indicates along with myriad three-dimensional items—spheroids, tetrahedrons, etc. Replicated designs, once a monumental bore for the designer, can be produced in a trice. Individual designs can be changed quickly and accurately, while differing configurations can be seen in full three-dimensional views.

That's CAD, computer-aided design. What about CAM—computer-aided manufacture? Numerical control tapes can be produced by these CAD systems to direct computer-controlled machine tools in manufacturing the product the computers have helped design.

CAD/CAM Does It Best

Obviously, such equipment costs more than pen and ink; more than manual production. But in terms of the savings involved, cost shrinks to relative insignificance. As a matter of fact, CAD/CAM systems can provide tenfold and, occasionally, fifteenfold gains in productivity. Even a two-to-one improvement in productivity allows typical investments to be recovered in remarkably little time.

Two-to-One Productivity Gains

Consider what a two-to-one gain in productivity would mean. Assume a manufacturer buys a stand-alone CAD/CAM system with four to six work stations and a minicomputer and that it costs $300,000—the norm not so long ago. If the new system chops in half the engineering time required to complete a design, the user realizes a gross return on investment that can pay for the CAD/CAM system in as little as two years. Tom P. Kurlak, a Merrill Lynch analyst, explains:

> A job requiring five engineers that manually would take six months and cost $100,000 in salary and overhead could be done in three months for $50,000 if the two-to-one productivity criteria were met. The saving of $50,000 is [about] 17 percent of the initial cost of the CAD/CAM system of $300,000.

But the 17 percent saving occurred over three months, one-fourth of a year. Mr. Kurlak adds:

> This gross return, before depreciation, annualizes to [just under] 67 percent, since within one year these five engineers can accomplish two years of designing for half of the manual cost of $400,000. This example of five engineers is fairly typical since most CAD/CAM systems are sold with five work stations.

Remember that in many applications the productivity gains can go as high as 10 to 15 times. And there is more to it even than that. Reduction in the product design cycle allows companies to get to market more rapidly with new products—critical in establishing or maintaining market share in many instances. Further, reduced design cost per product offsets continued materials inflation.

CAD/CAM is a dynamic business as are so many computer businesses in which a software package is important. Software can be altered and improved to reflect new needs and the considerable imagination of the sort of people who become computer systems analysts and the people who use the machines on the job. For example, during 1980, color displays gained momentum despite relatively inferior display techniques as well as a 3-to-1 cost disadvantage relative to monochromatics. Networking—whereby remote terminals are wired into a mainframe computer for higher data accuracy and additional software capability—is also emerging as a trend.

The Exploding Markets for CAD/CAM

Entire industries have welcomed CAD/CAM to meet production problems. For example, rising fuel costs and increased restrictions on pollution have stimulated the auto industry's demand for CAD/CAM systems. CAD/CAM offers a way out of otherwise insoluble problems. Similar challenges face the aircraft manufacturing industry, where CAD/CAM offers the only way possible to design today's sophisticated aircraft.

The electronics industry is another major market for CAD/CAM. The chief applications are the design of complex printed circuit board layouts and circuit design for semiconductors.

Governments and utilities are using CAD/CAM for mapping resources, facilities, street plans, pipelines, underground utilities, and zoning.

Oil and chemical companies use CAD/CAM for complex piping layouts in refinery and petrochemical plant designs.

The civil engineering field is a potential market and already uses computer graphics in large construction projects, structural design, and seismic mapping of mineral deposits.

Kurlak concludes that the demand for CAD/CAM systems is exploding, "broadly based and cost-justified by today's critical labor and materials productivity challenge." Kurlak comments that industry shipments in 1980 totaled about half a billion dollars and believes that growth can average 30 to 50 percent over the next several years. "This

CAD/CAM Does It Best

would produce an industry of $1.5 billion in sales by 1984 and rank it among the fastest-growing sectors of the economy."

CAD/CAM Candidates

There are a number of companies in the industry that have promise, from the acknowledged leader, vertically integrated Computervision, to recently acquired Applicon, the leader in the electronics market, to Auto-trol, whose emphasis in civil engineering has put it ahead of the pack in that field. Until recently anyway, Auto-trol's shares were offered over the counter, where first trading in a company's shares usually takes place. Dozens of other, smaller companies participate, but seven—the other leaders are IBM, Calma, Integraph, and Gerber Systems Technology—have a clear lead over the competition. Gerber, with 4 percent of the market the smallest of the leaders, does more business than all of the remaining suppliers combined except for IBM, which has 5 percent of the market.

CAVEAT: *As is so frequently the case in computer-related fields, the $64 million dollar question is: Will that colossus of the industry, IBM, plunge into the muddy CAD/CAM waters and, like a giant crocodile, swallow up all but the strongest swimmers? IBM has been offering a software package from Lockheed with a Sanders Associates graphics terminal tied to IBM mainframe systems already owned or leased by IBM customers. Tentative though its CAD/CAM thrusts have been so far, IBM has carved out a surprising market share at the expense of some leaders. IBM would be the natural supplier to major companies that already use its mainframes.*

Marketing Essential: Holding Share of Market

It is always important for the investor to watch a developing industry closely. For while earnings may grow rapidly enough to cause a stock to quadruple in price in a short while, such gains are unlikely to materialize—or having materialized are unlikely to hold—if the company begins to lose share of market. Lagging growth, as everyone knows, can trigger heavy sales on the part of investors who are determined to stay with the leaders. A company doesn't actually have to lose market share. It is enough that investors perceive that this is happening to send a stock downhill.

Computervision Draws the Markets

CONCEPT: *A dominant company plays from strength. Here's a study in leadership. Computervision is the largest producer of computer graphics systems in the world, with an estimated market share of 42 percent in 1980. It produces "turn key" equipment—the user unpacks it, plugs it in, and goes to work. There is no need to tie into other computers or even into a mainframe, as these machines stand alone.*

By market share standards, Computervision continues to gain and by a significant degree. The company had just 33 percent of the market in 1979. The second largest factor, Applicon, which has just become a part of Schlumberger, held its own in 1980 with 14 percent of the market. Calma, a new subsidiary of G.E., held 14 percent, Auto-trol, 10 percent, and Integraph a 10 percent share in 1980. Evans & Sutherland had about 7 percent of the market in 1980. Gerber (down from 5 percent to 4 percent) lost share to the leader, Computervision. (Auto-trol and Calma simply didn't have the manufacturing capacity to maintain their market share but revenue growth has accelerated for both as new capacity has materialized.)

Computervision is three times the size of Applicon, its closest competitor, and realizes twice the smaller company's pretax margin of profit on sales at 19.9 percent, the highest in the industry. Computervision's ability to bring dollars to the bottom line in part reflects the fact that it is the most vertically integrated concern in the industry, producing virtually all its own hardware except for the cathode ray tube screen and tape and disk drives. Its minicomputers are designed specifically for CAD/CAM applications.

CAD/CAM Does It Best

It's worth noting that IBM designs multipurpose computers, each doing a number of jobs well but not always as well in a given application as competitive equipment designed for a specific purpose.

Big Dollars for R&D

Computervision has the largest software staff in the industry. In fact, Computervision accounts for a third of the research and development money spent in the industry. If those R&D dollars help Computervision produce a quality product—and the evidence is that they do—then it is no wonder that this company is the one to beat. Obviously, in an industry growing as rapidly as CAD/CAM is, Computervision must be watched as carefully as any of its competitors for signs of lagging growth and possible market saturation, though neither seems a major concern at the moment.

Computervision is in several of the most important CAD/CAM markets and dominates more than one. Kurlak of Merrill Lynch estimates that Computervision commands 44 percent of the mechanical design market—more than three times the share of its nearest competitor. Computervision also has an estimated 36 percent of the electronics market, 20 percent of the civil engineering market, and 10 percent of the mapping market.

Kurlak concludes that the company's dominance in the most rapidly growing field, mechanical design, assures it of above-industry average growth over the next several years. Through its vertical integration the company maintains control over total systems performance. Yet the management is said to be flexible on hardware technology. Management has not committed itself to technologies that would prevent the company from using hardware advances produced by other companies.

Some Contenders

Merrill Lynch recently ranked the leading companies in terms of their relative excellence—looking at hardware, software, reliability, service, and overall quality.

They ranked as follows: Computervision, first; Calma and Applicon, tied for second; IBM, third; and Auto-trol, fourth.

Merrill Lynch concluded that Computervision was likely to sustain its large market share over time. They have long recommended Computervision as a buy—long term. The report added:

> Applicon, which tied with Calma (the latter recently acquired by General Electric), has been improving its position in the industry through aggressive marketing of substantially upgraded software packages. Its relatively low hardware rank should rise with the strong effort it has mounted in color raster displays, ink-jet plotters, and attached 32-bit processors.
>
> Auto-trol's lower ranking is affected by the small sample of users of its products represented here. However, its relative position is low in four of five areas, while IBM with a similarly small sample of users has only three areas of noted weakness. Since Auto-trol is just beginning to penetrate the three-dimensional, engineering-intensive market, its profile remains low at this time. We believe its position can therefore improve.

But the prime recommendation at Merrill Lynch in recent months is for Computervision, which has made such great strides. Obviously, though, the future of the stock is less certain. A cautious evaluation on that score states that there is a price for "all this progress."

The report notes that Computervision's achievements have attracted lots of trading interest and that yearly volume equals the 12.2 million shares outstanding. Further, not unlike the price-earnings ratios of other potential future stocks, the P/E of Computervision has been bid up to "a fancy level."

CAVEAT: *The report concludes: "With the normal multiple likely to be considerably less than the current one (the P/E was 34 at the time the analytical report was written), the stock has less potential for some time." The report added that the shares are 70 percent more volatile than the market as a whole. True. As this went to press the P/E ratio was down to 24 in the bear market of fall, 1981. Increasing competition from powerhouse IBM, which recently moved solidly into the industry's number two spot, leaves Computervision as CAD/CAM's only prospect for future stock status.*

CAD/CAM Does It Best

Faulty Perceptions on Wall Street

Experienced motorcyclists preparing to pass automobiles know that they must make motorists aware of their presence—particularly at intersections when the car may turn left without signaling. Hard as it may be to accept, motorists often do not *perceive* motorcycles in their rear-view mirrors. The motorist will, of course, see another car or a truck but motorcycles are simply not within the motorist's mind set. Assuming that the motorcyclist survives the resulting collision, he may face a driver who argues emphatically that he did not see the biker. And the driver will be telling the truth.

Faulty frames of reference block out the unexpected in Wall Street, too, and in important ways. Here's an important one for seekers of special situations—companies that will do better than the other participants in their field. As you know, Wall Street securities analysts are organized along industry lines with different analysts covering the various beats—weighing advantages and disadvantages of each company in the industry. The system works pretty well unless there's a company that by virtue of special attributes is so different from the rest that industry statistics are not an appropriate measure of its potential.

Harris to the Rescue

Invariably such companies are linked by the analysts with their slower-moving competitors. However successful the mutant, its shares may not sell at a deserved premium for years. It was some time, for example, before the restructured Harris Intertype Company, an old-line printing press and equipment company, was accurately perceived in The Street as a high-technology company—the successful producer of sophisticated word processing systems for newspaper writers, editors, and compositors. As mentioned earlier in this book, Harris shares experienced a spectacular advance once the company's metamorphosis was generally recognized.

CAVEAT: *By some key tests the play is over in Harris.*

Cross & Trecker: Born-Again Growth Company

Harris is not the only example of a born-again growth company. As this book went to press, a fine old machine tool company called Cross & Trecker was still perceived in Wall Street as a fine company, period. But Cross & Trecker was not perceived for what it is—a leader in CAM.

Yet, in Wall Street's view, Cross & Trecker isn't fundamentally different from any other machine tool company. Analysts persist in measuring Cross & Trecker in terms of machine tool industry expectations. If the industry could expect sales gains of x, then Cross & Trecker could expect to experience sales gains of similar dimension. Few recognized what Cross & Trecker had become through a merger in 1979. By joining machine builder Cross with a computerized-equipment maker, Kearney, the merged company was positioned to become a leader in computer-aided machine design and manufacture. Some believe the company will stand out among its competitors as the nation turns increasingly to automated factories.

No Ho-Hum Machine Tool Company

Securities analyst Joan M. Finsilver of the investment house of Fred Alger Management, Inc., argues that Wall Street analysts haven't perceived the significance of the merger of Kearny's capabilities in electronic controls with Cross's floor-long unmanned machine complexes.

Cross & Trecker itself said in a recent annual report, "We program into our products a computer-controlled maintenance capability, which enables our customers to correct machine malfunctions through a telephone connection to our diagnostic computers in Milwaukee."

Miss Finsilver points out that the electronics division—Kearney & Trecker—expects that its computerized equipment will soon be so sophisticated that "its machines will know when they are sick and will be able to affect their own cures."

The next step, regarded as inevitable in the years ahead, will be to make the machine complexes so flexible with software packages that

CAD/CAM Does It Best

they will turn out, say, valves and then engine blocks and so forth through myriad product changes. Miss Finsilver points out that:

> The problem has been that if you are manufacturing a high-volume part, the machine quickly pays for itself as it would in turning out engine blocks for General Motors. But if a part is produced in small quantity and it can't be produced on a machine that switches from one part to another, the capital investment involved is too high to provide a return for the manufacturer.

Rolling with the Punch Press

Programing the machines so that they can quickly shift to the production of different parts would solve that problem, she added. Cross & Trecker is working in that direction and is spending heavily to succeed. The company disbursed $4.2 million on research and development on sales of $350 million, or about 1.2 percent, in 1980 and doubled that R&D total in 1981, she said. Most machine tool companies spend much less, and almost no one is attempting to solve these problems as aggressively as Cross & Trecker. The company is "far and away the leader," in Miss Finsilver's view, a view shared by some other analysts. Few know and follow the company, it should be noted.

What's to Come

Miss Finsilver may be right in thinking that Cross & Trecker is a candidate for major gains in the years ahead. The shares may even become a future stock. But right or not, and whether or not the company experiences those gains, there can be no question but that highly automated factories will become an increasingly important part of the industrial scene, eventually dominating it. The Bureau of Labor Statistics has predicted that manufacturing's share of the national work force will shrink to 5 percent by the year 2000, down from nearly 25 percent in 1980.

Obviously, labor unions are concerned about the potential for massive loss of jobs. But in some nations such equipment has been added without loss to the labor force—so far, at least. Anyway, from an investor's point of view, the market potential is huge.

Little more than 1 percent of the nation's machine tools are equipped with rudimentary numerical controls using individual punched tapes to guide operations. The situation is bound to change. Even with the low level of automation generally, the United States has lagged behind Japan and most of Europe. What's more, the United States is beginning to experience shortages of skilled labor such as have resulted in growing automation in Europe and Japan.

Whatever happens, more automatic factories will arrive accompanied by pain in years to come. They have in the past. Caterpillar Tractor, while close-mouthed about an automated transmission-case plant in East Peoria, Illinois, acknowledged in 1978 that it was having considerable difficulty getting the plant to operate efficiently. The equipment, incidentally, was customized by Caterpillar itself. While the new plant turned out transmissions, it did not produce the necessary numbers. Full cost benefits were not achieved in the early stages, but it is currently producing cost savings above anticipation.

As for Cross & Trecker, the *Value Line Investment Survey* commented a while back: "One look . . . and you might think mergers are made in heaven. Since being formed via merger . . . this company has earned exceptional returns on equity. Net profits margins are hitting new peaks, with sales and earnings growing faster than ever before."

The company has moved into the twenty-first century with a healthy balance sheet. Debt constitutes a mere 2 percent of capital. If this sounds like a prosaic machine tool company, then Beethoven wrote "How Much Is That Doggy in the Window?"

Cross & Trecker's competitors include Joseph Lamb, a private company, and Snyder, which was private until purchased by Giddings & Lewis in 1981. The two companies are expected to have some of the synergistic benefits enjoyed by Cross & Trecker. Ingersol Milling Company, another private company, is also active in computer-directed manufacturing systems.

Others favor Condec Corporation, the Greenwich, Conn., high-technology company that owns Unimation, the largest robotics company. As one fan comments, "Someday Condec will sell off its junk [its

CAD/CAM Does It Best 117

less-promising divisions, and concentrate on Unimation]. It's an interesting but risky situation." At press time, Unimation was becoming a public company through an offering of almost one million shares.

CAVEAT: *Some believe that an important stock among publicly owned automated factory builders is yet to emerge and that when one does emerge, it won't be Cross & Trecker. In some ways Cross & Trecker does not resemble high-tech companies of great promise.*

SUMMARY: *Automation's twins, CAD and CAM, offer exciting potential for enhancing productivity for specific companies and for the nation as a whole. There are clearly several exciting companies with future stock potential among the builders of computer-aided design equipment. There is similar potential among builders of computer-aided manufacturing equipment, though the candidates for future stock growth in this area are not obvious. Most are older companies in the previously unexciting machine tool business.*

7

Long Shots in Solar Power

CONCEPT: *Long shots are as appealing in Wall Street as at the track. They don't win often, but when they do the payout can be extraordinary.*

Solar Power Through High Technology: Will It Short-Circuit the Power Companies Soon?

Long-shot candidate: The first company, or companies, to harness the sun through advanced solar cells would be in a position to exploit an almost limitless market for rooftop power. A number of old-line companies are in the race. If some giant company were to win the race, the feat would be analogous to a gambler's fantasy whereby venerable Affirmed comes out of retirement to win next year's Kentucky Derby against the year's best three-year-olds.

Corporations are like horses: Great old ones rarely have the potential of excellent young ones. That is, a company with sales of $1 million a year can move to $100 million more easily than a $5 billion company can move to $50 billion. But in rooftop solar power, so vast a market is suggested—with every house and trailer home a prospect—that one or more giant companies with a workable product could once again

Long Shots in Solar Power

become supergrowth companies. But again, to invest on that basis in a giant company is to speculate, though the speculation may not be near so risky as one in a small company.

Santa Claus on the Roof

For some reason—caution on the part of the press or the resistance of entrenched interests—major new technological developments characteristically are greeted with a skepticism that can persist even after a *fait accompli.* For example, Detroit continued to argue that Federal pollution control standards mandated for later in this decade were technologically unachievable long after Honda of Japan began producing an automobile with a "controlled charge" gasoline engine that met those standards.

The same "it can't but has been done" situation may apply to sun-fired household power. To wit, it is still being argued that major scientific and technological advances must be made before the direct conversion of sunlight into electricity can become a significant source of power. That was a position taken by a panel of scientists as recently as 1979 in a report to Federal energy agencies.

Were these scientists unaware or unimpressed with prior research by Texas Instruments? The answer is unclear. The fact is that a year and a half before the panel report was filed, that company's scientists led by Jack S. Kilby obtained key patents on a system that promised rooftop solar energy devices efficient enough to light and heat homes—even homes in northern latitudes. The system is so far along that some believe the system will be marketed by the middle of this decade.

If that seems farfetched, remember that the clue to the potential of this development came from Texas Instruments itself. In typically conservative fashion, Texas Instruments' management first spoke about the matter in a brief aside at the 1979 annual meeting, four years after the company obtained its first patent on the system.

Texas Instruments: Born-Again Growth Stock?

The revelation fascinated knowledgeable observers because Texas Instruments is a remarkable company. Incorporated in 1938 as Geophysical Service, Inc.—an energy exploration company that still provides such services—it became Texas Instruments in 1951. In 1947, Bell Labs invented the silicon transistor and baby Texas Instruments took over where Bell left off to become a predominant semiconductor producer. Currently, Texas Instruments is in the forefront of semiconductor and microprocessor technology. Its efforts run the high-technology gamut, through microwave ovens, computer memories, thermostatic and electrical components, undersea warfare signal studies, the space program, target detection and acquisition programs, missiles, specialized chemical materials, clad metals, and precision controls and switches. It is huge, employing nearly 87,000 people in 44 plants in 18 countries.

Texas Instruments is not just a well-run industrial company. It has employed shrewd pricing techniques in becoming a $4.5 billion company. That revenue base, incidentally, is more than double the $2.05 billion of 1977.

Down the Pricing Curve

Clearly, the company is an aggressive, hard-hitting organization. This shows even in its pricing policy. TI prices its new products in a manner designed to carve out a leadership position in the marketplace before would-be competitors can get underway. The technique, which is employed by some other high-tech companies, including microprocessor producers, is called "experience curve" pricing, under which reductions are made as quickly as manufacturing economies are achieved with growing output. The technique is markedly at odds with the method of pricing new products followed by old-line companies, where the price is kept at premium levels for highest returns while the product is unique in the marketplace.

Texas Instruments obviously shares the view of some pricing ex-

Long Shots in Solar Power

perts who argue that high initial prices invite competition and may reduce the innovator's total rewards substantially over the full life cycle of the product. Does it work? That superior innovator, Henry Ford, was one of the first to use experience curve pricing and it certainly worked for him. Henry Ford kept chopping the ticket on his Model T, thus managing to retain the lion's share of the new-car market for many years. Texas Instruments' pricing approach is offered to suggest that the company is progressive on many counts and to argue that this pricing method has worked for TI.

However, like Ford, TI has been slow to offer a range of products and this has cost TI market share.

Texas Instruments does not stint in important areas. Relatively speaking, Texas Instruments spends an enormous amount of money on research and development. Its 4.2 percent annual R&D expenditure compares with 3.6 percent for technology companies generally and 1.2 percent for all industry.

Jack Kilby: Inventor

Texas Instruments scientists are among the most accomplished in the nation. Team leader Jack Kilby is no visionary but one of the nation's top inventors, with over 50 patents in the field of integrated circuits. Newsletter writer and consultant Ben Rosen, who was perhaps the first analyst to guess at the potential of Texas Instruments patents in solar energy, notes that Kilby, along with Robert Noyce of Intel, holds the patent for the invention of the monolithic integrated circuit. The two men developed the same device independently. Mr. Kilby also holds one of the basic patents for the hand-held calculator, which he began to develop in 1966. Moreover, he is a principal inventor of thermal printing."

More to the point, says Rosen: Kilby not only has invented, but his inventions in several cases have created new industries: "Demonstrating esoteric and interesting scientific phenomena . . . may engender interest in specialized scientific circles and occasionally even in the press. But what's really hard to do is to create innovative, commercial products which can be economically produced."

When Texas Instruments mentioned solar energy at the 1979 annual meeting, the case was tactfully understated. The company showed a single slide while President Fred Bucy reported that the company was engaged in a promising solar energy conversion program. He said the approach seemed to attack successfully most of the shortcomings of alternate methods, and that a contract for four years worth $14 million had been obtained from the Department of Energy. Texas Instruments hasn't announced anything on the subject since.

Shine the Light over Here, Please

The design, details of which have been gleaned from patent applications and other materials, seems to reflect Mr. Kilby's known sense of the practical. In a number of key respects, the work by Mr. Kilby's team seems to overcome what are regarded as key stumbling blocks.

Like the other approaches, the TI-Kilby method (Mr. Kilby has retained a share of potential profits from the system) uses photovoltaic conversion—changing sunlight directly into electricity. But conventional solar cells—those pioneered in spacecraft and in use in a limited number of household collectors today—are prohibitively expensive.

A discussion of present techniques suggests why there is such skepticism in official circles with regard to the promise of solar power. Mr. Rosen has detailed the problems at length in his newsletters. For one thing, the so-called Czochralski method of producing the necessary silicon for the cells is slow, expensive, and erratic. Silicon ingots must be sawed mechanically, with an initial waste of half the silicon. If a more efficient electricity producer, gallium arsenide, is used, the cost of production "can be magnified as much as 100 times," says Rosen. Besides, there's arsenic in the compound—a highly poisonous substance and potential threat to the environment. Promising copper sulfide cells are also toxic. The less productive silicon cells are safe.

The idea of solar cells is to get more energy at less cost, of course. Rosen says that most observers tend to ignore the "energy input" side of the equation: "Depending upon which type of cell you use and whose estimates you believe, it takes anywhere from five to nine years to recover in electricity the energy that goes into a solar cell's manufac-

Long Shots in Solar Power

ture." Thus, mass production could actually exacerbate the nation's energy deficit.

Making the Connection

Once conventional solar cells are produced, they must be connected in parallel. Any defective cells seriously affect performance. Thus, reliability becomes a serious problem.

We sunbathe during the day, and so do solar cells. The light—the power source—is turned off at the end of the day as if by a switch as the sun drops below the horizon. But the solar power user may need even more power at night than during the day. Ergo, one of the many critical problems has been to store the electricity collected during sunny days for use during cloudy days and at night. The obvious but inadequate answer: batteries. They are expensive, take lots of space, and must be maintained.

As Texas Instruments has stated the problem, a photovoltaic breakthrough must meet a number of conditions: (1) It must offer reasonable conversion efficiency; (2) the components must be of readily available materials; (3) the process must offer integral energy storage; and (4) it must employ a manufacturing process that is "forgivable"—one that will turn out solar cells of high reliability and at relatively low cost.

Texas Instruments would appear to have met all these conditions with an integrated system that is highly innovative, even elegant. TI settled on silicon for its solar cells. After oxygen, silicon—a component of sand—is the most abundant material on the face of the earth.

Potent Beads of Power

As Ben Rosen explains, the TI process uses spherical cells 100 to 200 microns in diameter, as compared with the three-inch planar cells of the complex Czochralski method. The TI method of making the cells is remarkably similar to that used in making buckshot—an inexpensive process. It is the element in the Texas Instruments process that Rosen regards as the "big and novel breakthrough."

Doped silicon is melted in a tube and forced through a nozzle that sprays droplets which are allowed to fall a distance of eight feet. The silicon solidifies as it falls, forming spheroids. Unlike planar silicon cells, which must be produced with a high degree of precision, the kinds of imperfection that result in the spheroids as a result of this process are of no consequence.

Compare the TI beads with silicon wafers. Only 12 percent of the conventional planar cells will produce current, while nearly 95 percent of the spheres are productive.

Besides, defective spheres that are actually incorporated into the system can be tolerated. Since there are no connections among the spheres, there is no interdependence. A shorted cell won't affect overall performance to a degree that exceeds the contribution of that sphere. The TI patent notes that if 100 cells are immersed in the same electrolytic solution and 5 are out, you get 95 percent of the output otherwise available. Such a defect in a conventional system could lead to a catastrophic failure, as the planar cells are interconnected; thus the manufacturers must try for 100 percent performance. This kind of design requirement is extremely demanding and results in costly waste.

A Comforting Margin for Error

As Ben Rosen points out: The Texas Instruments system "essentially averages over hundreds of thousands of cells." In conventional systems, a solar cell panel is not fabricated unless all the individual cells successfully pass tests. In the TI system, one tests not the individual cells but only the final system.

Once the spheres are produced, they are sorted for size, and metal contacts are applied along with thin insulating coatings. Every other spheroid is assigned a positive pole role and the rest are made negative. Remember that unlike conventional solar cells, the beads require no external electrical connections. The spheroids are then spread onto sheets, like sand on sandpaper. The sheets are then placed in tubes, which are transparent. They are bathed with an electrolyte. The tubes are elliptical so that they will refract the sunlight onto the solar cells with optimum efficiency during the day. As the sun hits the solar tubes,

Long Shots in Solar Power

electricity flows through the electrolyte, and hydrogen is produced in compound as a hydride.

The safe hydrogen hydride remains in a cellar container to be used on demand to power a fuel cell that will produce the electricity needed for household use—even after the sun goes down. Fuel cells are highly efficient relative to batteries. While the quest for a better battery continues, fuel cells capable of the solar task are already available.

But what of the efficiency of the system—and how much roof space does it take? Today's solar panels generate 5.5 watts per square foot; four years from now, panels may generate 10 watts per square foot. (TI's solar panels are thought to be even more efficient.)

Power to the People

The typical household needs 15,000 to 20,000 watts a day. At 10 watts per square foot, that would require 1,500 to 2,000 square feet of roof, about the size of a typical roof. With storage facilities, panels covering less roof surface would do the trick. And there is a bonus item. Every solar system throws off considerable thermal energy that would help the economics of a photovoltaic system. The thermal energy can power a heat exchanger that will run such energy-gobbling devices as hot water and space heaters and even absorption-type air conditioners.

Rosen speaks of the economics of solar power—today and tomorrow. He notes that today one can buy 24-watt solar cell panels from Motorola at a cost of $13.67 per watt if the purchaser takes quantities of 500 panels. The panels, he says, will provide DC power of 25 volts and "have no integral storage capacity."

But when systems like Texas Instruments' are available commercially, he expects the cost per watt "to meet or fall below" the Department of Energy's target cost of 50 cents per watt. Not only is that 27 times lower than current costs, but there would be storage and co-generation of usable thermal energy as well. "At such a price, a residence could have its 20,000 watts of rooftop power supplied at a capital cost of $10,000, an amount which will probably be a pittance compared to projected 1990 home prices."

Electricity today costs from less than 5 cents per kilowatt hour in the Southwest to over 10 cents in the Northeast. Mr. Rosen notes that conventional photovoltiac schemes would become economic only if energy prices go even higher, as they probably will. But Texas Instruments' system appears to promise energy within today's 5 to 10 cents range.

Better Late Than Never

Don't count the days until Texas Instruments comes to market with this remarkable new product. It could happen in five years and it may take ten. Or, developmental problems may stall the system completely. In fact, corrosion problems of an unknown degree of seriousness may have developed in connection with the storage of the hydride.

It does seem, though, that Texas Instruments is on to something. And it does seem that Texas Instruments, a $4.5 billion company already, is likely to grow even without solar power at a rate equaled by few smaller companies. It is estimated that earnings in the next several years will grow at a 16 percent rate—enough to bring market rewards on a price-earnings ratio that is relatively low for high-technology companies. As for solar panels, if successful they could transform Texas Instruments into a supergrowth company. For the market potential is staggering. There are 70 million households, and if everyone bought a TI-type system at $10,000 an installation, that would amount to a $700 billion market. Obviously, TI would have competitors. Equally obviously, the company would use experience curve pricing, bringing the price ever lower as time progressed. Even so, the market would amount to one of the largest ever exploited.

Future Stock Seekers: Watch for the Departure of Key Designers from Major Companies

Though it may never happen, Texas Instruments is ripe for the departure of a design team such as the group that left Hewlett-Packard to form Tandem; and the Cray group that left Control Data to form Cray Research, both of which are discussed in the next chapter.

CAVEAT: *Obviously, Texas Instruments will discourage defections at all costs. The fact that the company's key man in solar research, Jack Kilby, has been with Texas Instruments for many years and shared in its success militates against this event—attractive though it would be for those interested in seeing the company's solar energy developed by a strong young company with more potential for major share gains than a $4.5 billion company with modest 15 percent annual earnings gain prospects. Texas Instruments is a well-managed company that beats off competition through innovation and aggressive pricing policies—sometimes cutting its own profits to do so. In any case, Texas Instruments hasn't made money for shareholders for years—the shares have been essentially static since 1973.*

A Hybrid Approach to Financing That Can Serve Seekers of High-Tech Profits in Major Companies

When Storage Technology, a Colorado manufacturer of computer peripherals, raised $50 million from wealthy private individuals in 1981, the company pioneered a means of obtaining capital that may someday offer a profitable new avenue for investors of modest means who seek high-tech profits.

Through Smith Barney Harris Upham, Storage Technology offered $150,000 participations in the development of a series of computer mainframes.

Those who bought units are speculating on the success of the project, hoping the reward will be several times what they put in and more than they might gain had they invested directly in Storage Technology's shares.

The limited partners have a Fortune 500 company behind them, yet are shooting for profits not unlike those associated with successful start-ups.

Other brokerage houses are interested in the approach as a possible major new financing technique. At press time, several deals were being structured for public offerings that would be available to individuals at $25,000 a unit.

If this approach becomes truly popular, a Texas Instruments might well finance its solar research on a basis that will offer added leverage for those who want a piece of the solar action but not the entire Texas Instruments package.

The Big Picture

SUMMARY: *In a larger sense, the investor should always recognize that high technology offers more promise today than ever before. Vast new markets are likely to result out of high-technology research in the years ahead. Some are likely to occur in energy, with biomass (plant) conversion into fuel an area of major interest. That is, renewable plant life may be a major factor in the production of fuel for automobiles someday—and without loss of foodstuffs. It is starch—not protein—that is useful for production of alcohol. Livestock can share the foodstuffs. (Note that Brazil has been converting its entire automobile fleet to use pure ethanol as fuel.) Meantime, high-technology medical, communications, and defense breakthroughs, among other areas, can lead to vast new markets. The investor should be alert to these research areas for potential future stocks.*

Part III

INVESTMENT STRATEGIES: HOW TO BUY AND, OCCASIONALLY, HOW TO SELL

STRESSING a point once again, this book is directed to long-term investors—not short-term traders. Thus, the reader need not be concerned about day-to-day—or month-to-month—market fluctuations. If the investor has picked well, the investor will be set for years—even if he or she pays a premium for shares relative to the company's current earnings, as explained in the next chapter.

The investor will be able to ignore, or at least put in perspective, temporary setbacks, as, for example, those experienced by Intel and Advanced Micro-Devices, each of which has posted diminished earnings lately. In fact, when negative news causes share price to decline, a buying opportunity may be created for the long-term holder.

Considering the question from a different perspective—when to sell—the wise investor may be able safely to delay that decision for years, even in a world of rapid-fire developments.

Remember that what investors are attempting to do in buying into the high-technology boom is to ride the future to gains reminiscent of those posted by high-technology shares over twenty years in the 1950s and 1960s—when such shares were up many times as much as the market generally.

Nevertheless, a book such as this one would be incomplete without guidelines suggesting what to pay on purchase and when to bail out. The remaining chapters address these topics in terms of several high-multiple stocks and in terms of technical means of evaluating share price.

8

When to Pay an Outrageous Multiple; What Tests to Employ

CONCEPT: *Normal share price evaluation tests often do not serve to identify future stocks. Investors in true growth companies can sometimes earn rich rewards even though they pay outrageous multiples of 30 times earnings or more. A copyrighted test employing growth in book value and rising return on equity points the way.*

For the cautious, the decision to buy shares at 20-plus price-earnings multiples is never an easy one. Careful weighing of the risks helps but does not guarantee success even when the investor is right. Remember that other holders are skeptical of high P/Es and may react to the slightest weakening of the company's growth rate. The first sellers in such circumstances are likely to be major institutional investors. In the rush to exit before other nervous holders, institutions may dump 100,000 shares in a single housecleaning trade. This is foolish, shortsighted, and suggests slavish attention to the number on the bottom line—the wrong focus, certainly for investors in future stocks. Temporary setbacks often interrupt a pattern of superior growth, a pattern that should resume in most cases and provide further major market gains in future. Nevertheless, share dumping is a factor to be reckoned with along the way.

Those who buy at high P/Es should be forewarned that they can be exposed to wrenching market setbacks. And any paper losses that may result can persist for months, perhaps causing the investor to doubt his judgment. Obviously, no long-term recovery will occur if, in fact, the market has accurately perceived a permanent slowdown in the rate of growth that caused the company's shares to carry a premium price in the first place.

Nevertheless, there are instances when high P/Es must be soft-pedaled as an evaluator, particularly so when the company in question has an unrivaled design and management team, and when such a company is also experiencing substantial growth in book value per share—the factor that correlates best with long-term growth in stock price—P/E sinks to relative unimportance.

Clearly, there are occasions when a computer builder or other high-technology company develops a product deemed by the marketplace to be without serious rival. If a company with such product is well managed, it may be able to exploit a captive market for years or move in on a previously developed market with deeply satisfying results for everyone concerned.

The pioneer may become king of the hill, so entrenched in the market that potential competitors will choose not to enter the arena. That's rare, though. Usually competition comes in. But even if it does develop, inroads against the entrenched innovator may be made only with the greatest of difficulty. For as we have seen, computer companies with unique products usually manage to establish long-term relationships with their customers; there is a high degree of "brand loyalty."

Let's consider cases in point. Both Tandem Computer and Cray Research seem to have achieved market dominance with unrivaled products in their respective fields and, as one might expect, the shares of these two small companies have soared. In fact, the shares of the two companies have reached such remarkable premiums relative to those of most other high-tech companies that only the most intrepid and knowledgeable of investors have dared to buy them lately. The shares of Rolm have also soared to the stratosphere. Rolm, like little David, has soared against the giant, AT&T.

On the Origin of Top Management

Tandem is a youthful company whose managers are mostly out of the brilliantly innovative, older high-technology company, Hewlett-Packard. One of Hewlett-Packard's successes has been its profit center approach, whereby it sets up smaller enterprises within the overall corporate framework. This method of inspiring initiative has its shortcomings. As the company-within-the-company begins to earn profits, the profit center managers may conclude that they can probably make a profit on their own. Defections are not uncommon and Tandem is an example of this.

It's worth noting that Hewlett's system of management undoubtedly enriches the American economy, but defections do not necessarily enrich Hewlett-Packard, which, nevertheless, scores high-tech profit gains of 18.5 percent a year. IBM, by contrast, nurtures its managers differently—in a way that may not sharpen basic profitmaking skills as much, though there have been IBM defections, too, à la Shared Medical Systems.

Tandem: The Computer That Never Breaks Down

The men who left Hewlett to found Tandem had concluded that in certain so-called "on-line" computer applications breakdown is intolerable. The "nonstop" computers that Tandem developed to solve this problem are a better mousetrap that has brought many Fortune 500 companies to Tandem's door.

No one who must operate computers 24 hours a day without pause would be impressed if a manufacturer promised 98.8 percent reliability. For example, what hospital using computers to monitor intensive care would be happy with that kind of performance?

But over the years, thousands of businesses with somewhat less demanding needs have installed systems that delivered 98.8 percent of the time, thinking that they had purchased virtual nonstop performance. Soon many of these users discovered to their chagrin that they had not purchased perpetual performance—nor even sufficient reliability to conduct business efficiently.

The customer learned that if a system failed once a month and was down for eight hours, the system still met that seemingly desirable 98.8 percent reliability specification.

But a full shift of downtime once a month was intolerable—even devastating—to many businesses. Thus, it became clear that insofar as some users are concerned, computer systems offering anything less than 100 percent reliability were unsatisfactory and might possibly preclude a company's computerization—unless, of course, complete paper records were kept as well. By analogy, then, a hand soap that is ninety-nine and forty-four one hundredth's percent pure may be pure enough and to spare for human use, but a computer of similar reliability could be and probably would be highly unsatisfactory in some important applications.

Tie Them Together and Hope

There is much more to the story in a business world in which networks of computers tie many offices and plants together. In such instances, reliability may be a great deal worse than 98.8 percent performance suggests—particularly so for global companies with far-flung branches wired into a central data processing system.

Let's say that the main office of a stockbroker with a system offering 98.8 percent availability decided to tie the system into other branches. The broker would link the first computer with a similar unit in a remote location, thus beginning a distributed data processing network. Let's say that the second unit also offered 98.8 percent availability with that setup. Downtime builds dramatically.

The network would go off-line twice a month, or once every 15 days. With a third system tied into the network, the business would be "off the air" once every ten days, and with a ten-system network the business would be out every third day. Thus the reliability of systems with hundreds of stations each offering 98.8 percent performance becomes an unpleasant joke.

Computer customers have grown sophisticated and are fully aware

When to Pay an Outrageous Multiple; What Tests to Employ   135

of this phenomenon. Once they became convinced that a nonstop technology existed, they were prospects for the Tandem system. For the past five years or so Tandem Computers has been meeting that demand almost without competition and has prospered ever since.

Perpetual Motion Computers

Like many other manufacturers, Tandem Computer produces on-line computer systems. On-line systems permit the user to obtain data from the computer memory the instant it is logged in from any terminal. For example, the reservations clerks of airlines with on-line systems can tap seating requests into interconnected terminals and be informed instantly if there are seats left on individual flights (even if a number of terminals are asking for data at the same time). If the last available seat on a particular flight has been booked by, say, a Cleveland reservation clerk just milliseconds earlier, the clerk in Hawaii would get a no-seats message and inform his prospect that seating would be available on a standby basis only. This, of course, assumes that the airline's computer system was not down for repairs.

There are dozens of other businesses that operate in an on-line environment that requires perpetual performance and, equally important, accuracy. Banks use on-line teller stations and automated teller machines. For a bank, the consequences of malfunction can be severe as, for example, when a bank does a million-dollar electronic fund transfer. Suppose the bank forwards the money to the wrong place through computer malfunction?

Merchants use on-line services to provide instant authorization for credit card purchases. Manufacturers and distributors use on-line data systems so that they can give customers an instant status report on their orders. And, to quote Tandem, "There are scores of other businesses, hundreds of other users where the need to instantaneously and continuously access and update information is becoming vital. . . . In these businesses, when the computer stops—or when a computer malfunction damages or destroys the data base—the business stops."

The Day the Computer Bombed Cleveland

Tandem didn't offer this example, but Wall Streeters will recall that an important data base was destroyed in Ohio not so many years ago. The computer was in the Cleveland office of a major brokerage firm. One day it "bombed" without warning, wiping out unduplicated data in the computer memory. Embarrassed securities salesmen in that office had to send customers to rival brokers in the city. Meantime, the firm began a monumental effort to restore customer records through paper invoices and written records of customer trades. The result was far from perfect and, needless to say, lasting damage was done to the broker's business. Similar though less dramatic computer breakdowns in the early 1970s were common in Wall Street. Brokers were unable to match orders with other firms in thousands of cases. Several firms went under as a result, and a computer-based house of cards nearly collapsed. Had the collapse occurred, it is widely believed that a depression would have resulted.

Tandem's Solution

Obviously, Tandem Computer's founders were aware of these monumental risks, and the company set out to build computers through a new architecture in hopes of answering the need.

Tandem explains: "Unlike the typical multiprocessors of preceding generations, the Tandem system is not functionally redundant, all elements of the system are handling the workload, and no one processor is merely waiting for another to fail."

The "fault tolerant" architecture was novel when Tandem developed it and, at this writing, is still unique, though there is every reason to believe that Tandem eventually will face stiff competition from a number of rivals. By that time, though, Tandem is very likely to be entrenched in a major segment of the computer market.

Tandem Leads the Way

Among the company's boasts: Only Tandem systems can be geographically dispersed in a distributed data processing network without modifications to the hardware and without reprograming—extending benefits of uninterrupted operations, data integrity, and modular expansion to large, high-volume networks. Its various software products, says Tandem, enable users to establish distributed data processing networks with "much greater ease, speed and economy than ever before known in the industry."

With "EXPAND" network operating system, users can build a distributed data processing network of up to 255 geographically dispersed Tandem systems without replacing hardware or changing applications software. Tandem believes the on-line computer market is a multibillion-dollar one and that it is growing at a rate in excess of 30 percent per annum. Tandem regards itself as the premier contender in this market.

Tandem, as the reader might expect, has been discovered by Wall Street and the shares carry one of the highest price-earnings multiples among the high-tech stocks.

Even so, as measures of value will show in a later chapter in this book, Tandem may still be an affordable future stock. The investor must examine the fundamental business prospects.

CAVEAT *(of general significance): Morgan Stanley notes that Tandem is still a relatively small company, though revenues will soon pass through the "psychologically important" $100 million revenue threshold. Morgan Stanley comments: "A number of technology-driven companies have stumbled as they emerged from entrepreneurial origins into a more structured corporate environment—a point in time which often has been defined as beginning at a revenue level of approximately $100 million. We believe that Tandem's management team, which includes [several former] senior Hewlett-Packard executives, is capable of leading the company on the path of continued high growth without serious missteps on the way.*

However, there are bound to be some anxious moments as one or another of the original members of the management team may leave or be replaced, or as a technical product problem leads to a quarterly earnings aberration. . . . The valuation of Tandem common shares appears to discount the company's high future earnings growth, possibly leaving little room for immediate appreciation."

Morgan Stanley's analysts, the husband and wife team of Ulric and Frederica Weil, went on to say that while they were not "valuation experts," with small, high-growth technology companies it does not pay to quibble over P/Es if the other factors—product excellence, market acceptance, and quality of management—are in place.

Tandem is not heavily leveraged. The balance sheet is essentially free of long-term debt. Note: Tandem might grow even faster with addition of debt. Convertible debentures could help Tandem hold share of market if tough competitors offer a challenge in years to come.

The Cray Advantage

Cray Research, whose founder was a research whiz at Control Data Corporation, has marched into a different segment of the computer world—the relatively small world of supercomputers, where profits are elusive.

When Seymour R. Cray left Control Data to found Cray Research in 1972, his stature in the research and investment communities was high enough that he obtained the necessary financing (despite records of losses by larger companies) and enough initial orders to guarantee profitable operation.

Cray Research turned the corner in just five years of corporate life, and with the sale of a single unit. To some who knew Cray and his research team, this came as no surprise. Cray brought several of his fellow designers at Control Data with him. In all, the Cray designers had more than a half a century of experience in large scientific computers. Incredible though it seems, Cray designers accounted for more than half the supercomputer experts in the world.

When to Pay an Outrageous Multiple; What Tests to Employ 139

This concentration of talent helps explain why design and development work leading up to Cray's first delivery cost the company just $8.5 million. The first sale—the company's second delivery since the first computer was leased—brought in $9 million.

Cray computers are massive in terms of their computing power but small in size. As the West Coast brokerage firm Montgomery Securities has noted, in the two years through fall 1980, Cray's toughest competitor, Control Data, managed to secure only two orders for its Cyber 203 against the 15 orders its rival received for the Cray 1.

The massive, room-sized Control Data supercomputer has since been redesigned as the Cyber 205—while improvements have caused redesignation of its rival as the Cray 1 S.

Control Data claims the 205 is eight times faster than its 203. If so, its power would be roughly equivalent to that of the Cray 1 S. At its basic price, Cyber 205 is cheaper, too. The Cray 1 S costs from $4.3 million to $13.5 million, depending on equipment and discounts.

Montgomery Securities analyst James R. Berdell says the Cyber 205 was bid against Cray several times and the Control Data Cyber was chosen only once in direct competition. He adds that while several hardware and software enhancements are planned for the Cray 1 S over the next two years, Cyber 205 still lacked a Fortran compiler in 1980—"crucial," in his view, for significant market penetration.

Thus, while it is reasonable to expect Control Data to win some orders on a price basis and/or more immediate availability in the future, Berdell does not believe the enhanced Cyber 205 to be a serious threat to Cray. He adds that the Cray 2, presently under development, will have five times the power of the Cray 1. Thus, he views competition from Control Data as healthy but "not significant." Cray is expected to deliver the Cray 2 in the mid-1980s for a slightly higher price.

Mini-Markets for Supercomputers?

CAVEAT: *The most important criticism one can make of Cray's prospects is the fact that the market for its supercomputers is limited.*

There are only 80 to 100 identifiable customers for supercomputers. Cray has already penetrated about 20 percent of that user base. But the customer base appears to be expanding at a 30 percent a year rate as businesses and governments begin to recognize that supercomputers provide a practical means of tackling the ever more complex problems of modern business. What's more, it is already clear that some current users will need more than one supercomputer.

As the market for these powerful machines develops, Cray seems to be proving as IBM did with mainframe computers many years ago that the market is substantially larger than anybody—including the marketing people at IBM—had imagined.

Investors should concentrate on the fact that it takes relatively few sales in the megabuck supercomputer market to build a respectable volume. Unfortunately, though, uneven sales can derail earnings temporarily. When that happens, some nervous holders may bail out.

And they did, too, in the second quarter of 1980. In the first quarter of 1980, the Cray installed two of its Cray 1 supercomputers and earned 55 cents a share. In the succeeding no-sale quarter, the company lost money—less than a penny a share. When it became clear that there would be no sales in the second quarter, the shares dipped, presumably because foolish investors took the short-term view. In any case, share price is much higher now and so are profits. Meantime, the stock has been split three for one.

What do these machines do, anyway? What makes them so valuable and so costly? Among the applications is weather forecasting.

There is an old story about a giant computer that offered daily weather forecasts—in 27 hours. Hardly timely enough to help one decide whether to take rubbers and umbrella to work. Forecasting with reasonable accuracy requires an immense number of calculations, calculations measured in the hundreds of trillions. If IBM's large, general-purpose CPU complex were employed for this task, it would take the computer until tomorrow to finish. The Cray 1 will produce a weather report in, say, 27 minutes or so. It should be noted, though, that reports prepared by the Cray 1 would be based on a relatively small "grid,"

When to Pay an Outrageous Multiple; What Tests to Employ 141

or overview, of the northern latitudes where United States weather usually originates. The reports are thus somewhat inaccurate—unless lots of Cray computers are used.

In a telephone interview Cray's Peter Appleton Jones, vice president of marketing, said that the next generation of Cray computers will gather and process information from a large-enough grid to provide accurate forecasts in a few minutes.

Cray supercomputers are also used in nuclear research, petroleum exploration, fluid dynamics, aerospace applications, engineering work, and in structural analysis.

Perhaps it takes a mathematician to understand the awesome power of the Cray computers. But this should help: The Cray 1 computer can execute over 240 million floating point operations per second (FLOPS). The Cray 2 may be capable of performing 1 billion FLOPS, while IBM's forthcoming general-purpose H series may achieve up to 105 million FLOPS.

(The Morgan Stanley analysts who made these calculations note that IBM's H series computers at $12 million will cost significantly more than the Cray 1 supercomputer in standard format. Nevertheless, the H series may be worth the cost, too. For while Cray's supercomputers are specialized, and dedicated to specific scientific tasks, IBM's equipment is versatile, capable of a wide range of commercial, scientific, and mixed applications. This, says Morgan, may justify IBM's higher unit price. But it won't win the specialized supercomputer market for IBM.)

Cray's success is due, as Morgan Stanley sees it, to excellence of design and—this is critical for Cray and other highly successful technology companies—the fact that Cray resisted the temptation to enter related computer markets. Say the Weils:

> [Cray quickly] established a high reputation for performance and reliability. Last but not least, Mr. Cray's decision to pursue the large-scale scientific market exclusively, despite what some perceived as rather limited market potential, has kept management's attention riveted on meeting the challenges of this demanding set of customers.
>
> By keeping the company small, cohesive, and devoted to one specific

task, management has avoided the design and manufacturing delays often caused by stifling bureaucracy and overlapping authorities. At the same time, the dedicated efforts of a small but highly qualified design team resulted in very good productivity at a surprisingly reasonable cost. Competitors often put a battalion to work to compensate for lack of genius, with mediocre performance the inevitable result.

Cray has another advantage. The company's business comes mostly from government or government-related departments and agencies (including the military) or from such recession-resistant industries as petroleum, aerospace, and high technology. The state of the general economy is rarely a factor for Cray's progress.

Recently, Cray has increased lease business. As a result, this business will contribute nearly half the revenue by 1982, up from 38 percent in 1979. Thus Cray's quarterly revenue stream promises to become much less volatile and more manageable than it is today.

Cray has long-term debt but not overmuch—about 20 percent of capitalization.

As John Hartwell, a money manager in New York City, comments:

> Cray may deliver fewer than a dozen computers in a year. With so few units, Cray can in effect "manage" its earnings. It makes a terrific difference whether an individual supercomputer installation is booked as a lease or a sale. Cray is leasing more and more and this defers the big profits to the end of the lease period. Everyone who really follows this company knows that its earnings are a half-truth that conceals the actual result. In a few years Cray will be posting fantastic numbers.

And Then There Was Rolm

We see that infant companies with top design teams can establish dominance in markets—even create new ones. But a spectacular example of marketing chutzpa is that of Rolm, which has succeeded—so far at least—against the largest competitor of them all, American Telephone & Telegraph. "Telephone" by some important measures is the biggest industrial company in the world.

Here's the background. Frequently a major manufacturer will for

When to Pay an Outrageous Multiple; What Tests to Employ 143

valid marketing reasons stay with an outmoded product, providing it to a customer who is satisfied that nothing better exists. It may be marketing hearsay but sewing machine manufacturers in this nation reportedly sold machines here after World War II that were obsolete in the European market, where Singer competed with state-of-the-art machines. With little competition here, Singer could sell the obsolete models in volume.

Similarly, American Telephone allowed its delivered product to lag technologically, partly, it appears, because AT&T was a monopoly and partly due to tax considerations. At any rate, Telephone's monopoly position was shattered in the 1960s when Carterphone won an antitrust suit against the communications giant. The upshot of the Carterphone decision was that customers could buy or lease telephones and other equipment from other suppliers if they chose to do so and hook them up to American Telephone lines. Ever since, dozens of companies have attempted to grab a piece of this lucrative market. The landscape is littered with corpses. Carterphone, having won its signal victory, was unable to build a significant base of business.

Obviously, American Telephone is still formidable and, besides, Telephone got there first—everyone uses Ma Bell's lines. Nevertheless, one late arrival has thrived. To an unusual degree Rolm Corporation has been able to capitalize on American Telephone's cumbersome size. A key point: Bell must move relatively slowly in improving its equipment, which is almost universally rented in business applications, else customers will demand the new equipment before the old is written off.

Rolm's special telephone equipment is being installed mostly in headquarters offices of Fortune 500 companies. In contrast to the agonizingly slow AT&T updates, Rolm can upgrade within days of innovation. That is, the new product "overlays" the old—new software, for example, can give added ability to control telephone costs. The control of telephone costs is the main benefit that Rolm offers to its customers.

Basically, Rolm gives customers three capabilities that previously were unavailable. First, Rolm equipment reduces access to long-distance lines by unauthorized personnel. Second, Rolm equipment automatically routes calls over the least costly transmission system—whether by microwave network or Bell lines. Third, Rolm equipment gives detailed reporting on telephone usage to identify employees who are using long-distance lines excessively.

Anyone who has watched fellow employees chatting with personal friends by telephone during business hours knows that significant corporate losses are involved. Rolm advertises that it can save as much as a third of a customer's toll charges the first year of installation.

While it may seem that Rolm has a limited market in the Fortune 500 companies, new generations of equipment are being developed constantly, and this means additional revenues for Rolm.

Eventually, Rolm is expected to begin competing with AT&T for the business of much smaller companies, including those with as few as 100 employees in one location.

How did a start-up company manage to grow enough to compete? It has been said that the assets walk out the door of some companies at the end of each business day. This is true at Rolm. Rolm's design team is its most precious asset. An industry observer, Boston consultant Donald W. Mitchell, comments that this vital design team is comprised of "a mere six people [who are] essential to the company's success."

The six come from Hewlett-Packard and other high-tech companies. They have, Mr. Mitchell insists, created "every innovation in this marketplace over the past several years."

CAVEAT: *"Were the design team to break up, the rate of new product introduction would slow substantially."*

Rolm is also known for computer systems, used by the military at rugged, remote sites. The computers intercept and analyze data, and jam enemy radar, among other military applications. Meanwhile the equipment can withstand severe environmental conditions found in such nonmilitary sites as offshore drilling platforms.

Once again, the problem is that Rolm is widely recognized for its accomplishments, and at price-earnings ratios in excess of 30 at times, the stock seems to have discounted a brilliant future. But who knows? Like many another high-technology company, Rolm could be a future

When to Pay an Outrageous Multiple; What Tests to Employ 145

stock. The reader will have to judge—in the context of two-for-one splits in each of the years 1978, 1979, and 1980. Some believe the company, with revenues of $200 million in fiscal 1980, will reach billion dollar status by the mid-1980s. Rolm will have to do so with rather larger debt than most future stock candidates. Its long-term borrowings constituted 52 percent of capital.

Tests: Fundamentals First, Then the Numbers Game

Shortly after the shares of the burgeoning home computer manufacturer called Apple were first offered to the public, they began to trade at a price-earnings multiple of 100. Theoretically, at least, this was not fatal to future success in the stock market. But analysis of the company in terms of total valuation and in terms of its competitors' market share at those prices was breathtaking, to say the least. And it is instructive to investors who are tempted to pay an unusually high price for high-technology shares. At a P/E of 100, a convincing argument can be made that Apple was too dear, despite the company's obvious prospects for high growth. The argument can be made on a fundamental basis as well.

Fundamentally Overvalued?

Apple Computer is one of the Horatio Alger stories of our time. It is run by uncommonly gifted young men who pad around the Apple premises in sneakers and jeans rather than the gray flannel suits preferred by the establishment. Yet it is widely agreed that these young men are building on a solid base. The Apple computer is an exceptional piece of equipment and is aimed at the exploding personal computer market. Not only do some experts expect to see a computer in most homes by the end of the decade, there are those who believe that millions of householders will own two or more computers by the year 1990.

Thus, when Apple shares were marketed at $22—under the auspices of that sage high-tech broker, Hambrecht & Quist—it is perhaps understandable that the shares reached 29 that same day. Soon after they were to sell at 34, or 100 times then-current fiscal year earnings of 24 cents a share. At that price, Apple also sold at 60 times estimates of 60 cents a share for fiscal 1981.

But rudimentary analysis would suggest that Apple could be ahead of itself in the stock market. With 62 million shares valued at 34, Apple Computer carried a total market capitalization at the beginning of 1980 of $2.1 billion. That's substantially more than Warner Lambert at $1.6 billion. Its market capitalization even puts Apple in the same ballpark with entrenched Sony Corp., which, not just incidentally, has developed a variety of small computers, variations of which will find their way into the home market. Still, at the time Apple sold at 100 times earnings, the market gave Sony a total market capitalization of only half again as much at $3.2 billion. More to the point, let's compare Apple with its more immediate rival, Tandy corporation.

Tandy Is Dandy

While Apple's computers must be sold by independent retailers who also stock a full selection of competitive home computers, Tandy has a total of 7,700 Radio Shack stores worldwide—including 125 that offer computers only.

Apart from Tandy's impressive retailing clout, Tandy personal computer business is larger than Apple's and is growing even more rapidly. While Tandy's total market capitalization is a little larger than Apple's, Tandy's price-earnings multiple was only 16 on estimated earnings of $1.50 a share when Apple commanded a P/E of 100.

Tandy offers many other electronic products, which do not equal personal computers in profitability. But Tandy's power in the retail marketplace is probably worth more than whatever software and technical superiority Apple may have. Obviously, then, Apple does not have unchallenged superiority in its basic market à la Tandem or Cray Research.

What's more, as we have already indicated, virtually every company—no matter how excellent the product line—inevitably faces severe growing pains when its revenues reach $100 million.

Apple's revenues reached $117 million in the fiscal year ended Sep-

When to Pay an Outrageous Multiple; What Tests to Employ 147

tember, 1980. Will this entrepreneurial company enter the more structured world of big business without tripping? That, too, remains to be seen.

While the company may be a great one, so far Apple has been a fad stock, not a future stock. Remember that great companies—as, for example, that wonderful high-technology company, American Telephone—do not necessarily make great investments.

Different Strokes for Special Folks: Market Cap/Over Revenues

Obviously, though, the raw P/E figure is not always helpful in making an investment decision about a high-technology stock.

When the price-earnings ratio moves through the roof, it is sometimes helpful to check how many times total market capitalization exceeds revenues. If that figure is more than three, the investor should ask himself whether he is being realistic about share prospects. Barring extraordinary circumstances, unreality may have set in. That test applied to Apple Computer is devastating. Apple shares at $2.1 billion total were selling at 18 times revenues.

On the other hand, Cray Research is also premium-priced by that test. With 13.6 million shares outstanding and a price of 30 at the beginning of 1981, total market valuation was over $408 million. Sales were $60 million. Thus Cray sold at nearly seven times revenues.

Tandem was also premium-priced by that test. With 4.2 million shares and a price of 70 in January, 1981, total market valuation was nearly $300 million. With 1980 sales of $109 million, Tandem sold at three times revenues. Rolm, with a market capitalization of $680 million and sales of $200 million, was still high at 3.4 times revenues.

The P/E Deflator: Putting Those Lofty P/Es in Perspective

Here's a method Wall Street analysts use to quantify earnings growth for stocks with high price-earnings ratios: They relate growth-to-P/E of the richly valued stock to growth-to-P/E of the Standard & Poor 500 stocks. If the relative growth of the richly valued stock is higher than that of the S&P, its high P/E may well be justified. But if the relative growth is lower, it isn't.

Here's how it works. Suppose the average earnings growth of the S&P stocks is 16 percent and the average price-earnings ratio is 8; divide 16 by 8 for an index number of 2. Suppose the high-tech stock's earnings growth is 40 percent and its price-earnings ratio is 20; divide 40 by 20 for an index of 2. Conclusion: The high-tech stock is no bargain relative to the S&P.

But if earnings of the high-tech stock are growing at an extraordinary 70 percent rate a year and the shares are selling at a price-earnings ratio of 30, its index is 2.33. The high-tech stock is cheap relative to the S&P at 2. Any index number in excess of that of the S&P suggests a stock is in buying range.

Obviously, if the general market declined so that the price-earnings ratio of the S&P was a bit over 5 while earnings growth remained constant, the index number would rise to 3. The high-tech company would have to grow even faster—at a 90 percent a year rate—even to justify a price-earnings ratio of 30.

This test has obvious shortcomings. Anyone employing it should be aware of fundamentals in his high-tech prospect—be sure the earnings result was not a fluke, for example. Moreover, the investor must keep in mind that any stock selling at a P/E ratio of 30 is likely to be volatile—subject to erratic stock market performance. The least disappointment can cause heavy selling.

The Rowe Price 2:1 Ratio Rule: Testing Relative Value of Growth Stocks

John Westergaard, whose Equity Research Associates is now an arm of Ladenburg Thalman & Co., Inc., has been a specialist in high-growth shares for many years. He offers a test of relative value for what he calls "junior growth stocks" versus the general market by making a comparison with the results posted by junior growth stocks over the past 20 years. In establishing his universe of junior growth shares, Westergaard uses the performance of the Rowe Price New Horizons Fund, that of similar funds, and that of Equity Research selections.

When to Pay an Outrageous Multiple; What Tests to Employ

There is, he says, a consistent relationship between the P/E ratio of junior growth stocks and the major averages depending upon the market psychology of the day. During bear market bottoms, the ratio of general market to junior growth P/Es tends to be one to one, and at bull market peaks, the ratio will tend toward two to one.

As the chart measuring the P/E ratio of New Horizons Fund versus the S&P 500 index shows, during the bear market bottoms such as 1962 and 1974, the P/E ratio of the fund was near a one-to-one ratio with the S&P index. When a change in ratio occurred, it tended to persist for an extended period of time, says Westergaard.

> Thus, following the bear market of 1962 the ratio hung at approximately 1.1 to 1 until mid-1965, at which point it began an extended rise. In 1974 the ratio broke down again to 1.05 to 1 and actually proceeded to decline to less than 1 to 1 in early 1977, at which point the ratio began an advance which carried it to 1.7 to 1 in late 1981.

Mr. Westergaard went on to point out that this did not mean that the Rowe Price junior growth stocks were losing ground in the stock market between 1974 and 1977, only that the rate of earnings gains for the juniors when compared to their market gains was greater than the rate of earnings gains for the major averages relative to their stock performance. That is, the fundamental (earnings) performance of the "juniors" outpaced their stock market performance.

As for the P/Es for all stocks historically, since the beginning of this century the ratio of the major averages has ranged from about 7 at the bottom (and briefly below that level) to 21 at the top. The average P/E since the turn of the century has been 14.

Notes Westergaard, "We also know that the P/E ratio of the major averages has tended to rise in long-term bull markets at the rate of approximately one multiple per year." Mr. Westergaard, like many others, is bullish on stocks and particularly so on junior growth issues.

Westergaard notes that in late 1980 the P/E ratio for the main averages—the 30 Dow Jones industrials and the S&P 500—was 8.3. At that time, Westergaard projected that they would add five multiples between that date and 1985. That would bring the P/E to 13.3. "We also state for the sake of argument, that junior growth stocks will gain

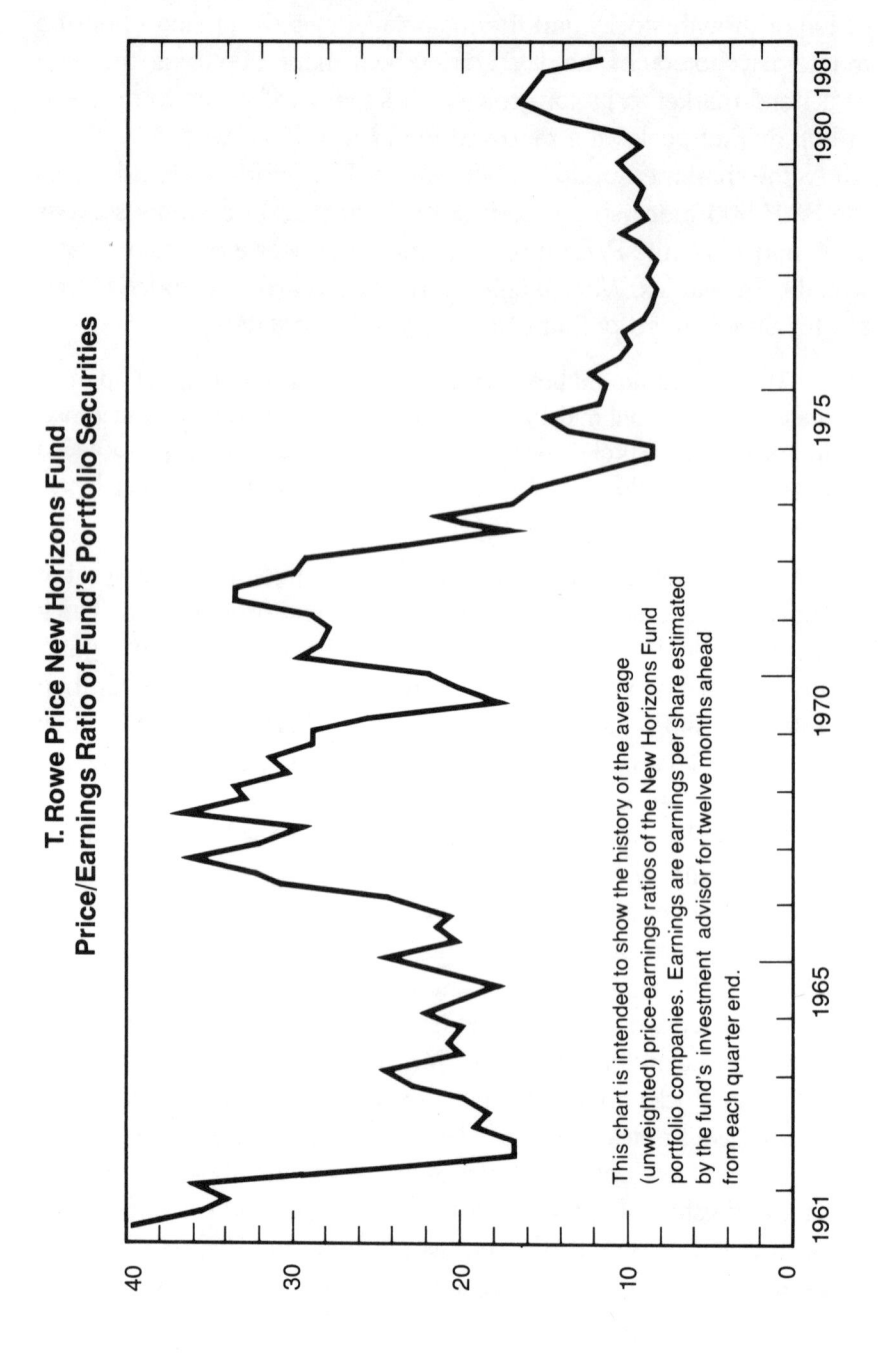

150 Investment Strategies: How to Buy and, Occasionally, How to Sell

T. Rowe Price New Horizons Fund
Price/Earnings Ratio of Fund's Portfolio Securities

This chart is intended to show the history of the average (unweighted) price-earnings ratios of the New Horizons Fund portfolio companies. Earnings are earnings per share estimated by the fund's investment advisor for twelve months ahead from each quarter end.

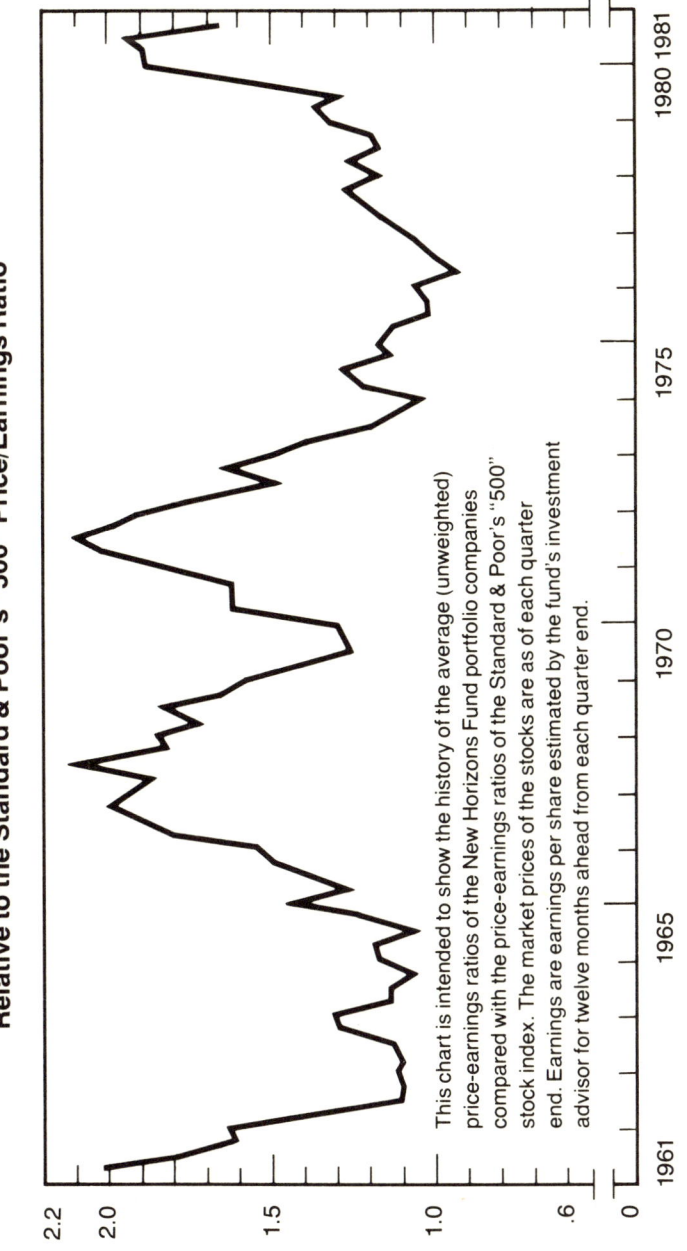

When to Pay an Outrageous Multiple; What Tests to Employ

T. Rowe Price New Horizons Fund
Price/Earnings Ratio of Funds Portfolio Securities
Relative to the Standard & Poor's "500" Price/Earnings Ratio

This chart is intended to show the history of the average (unweighted) price-earnings ratios of the New Horizons Fund portfolio companies compared with the price-earnings ratios of the Standard & Poor's "500" stock index. The market prices of the stocks are as of each quarter end. Earnings are earnings per share estimated by the fund's investment advisor for twelve months ahead from each quarter end.

in P/E ratio at the rate of 2½ times that of the major averages. This is more or less an arbitrary assumption based on historical reference and recent experience. Thus, we come to a projected pattern of P/E ratios as follows:

	1981	1982	1983	1984	1985
S&P	9.3	10.3	11.3	12.3	13.3
Jr. Growth Stocks P/E	15.8	18.3	20.8	23.3	25.8
Rowe Price 2:1 Ratio	1.7	1.8	1.8	1.9	1.9

If Westergaard's assumptions are correct, then a level of valuation wherein the "juniors" would be selling at 2 times the "majors" would not be achieved until 1985 or possibly 1986.

Westergaard finds the markets to be "increasingly volatile" and thinks they will continue so as the level of speculation increases. "There will be at the very least intermediate buy and sell points along the way."

Observation: There will be major breaks in the market from time to time and such breaks will offer excellent opportunities for purchasing future stocks at attractive levels.

The Seldom-Traveled Avenue to Riches: High Returns and Value Added

CONCEPT: *Growth in book value per share has the single biggest correlation with long-term growth in stock price. Yet some high-tech companies unconsciously pursue policies that retard increases in book value. In fishing for future stocks, look for gains in book value plus a sudden jump in return on equity.*

Mitchell and Company, Cambridge, Mass., consultants, have copyrighted this rising-book to high-return method of assessing underlying company values.

Unlike most other methods of gauging values, this one works. It cuts through the price-earnings ratio fog to offer a clear means of discovering when stocks are poised for supergrowth. It also suggests when to sell—the timing is critical and can protect hard-won profits.

Prime-Time Investing

For a few alert investors with an unerring sense of value, Prime Computer was a bargain in 1977. Incorporated in 1972 by former executives of Honeywell, Inc., Prime Computer was another, well, prime example, of the sort of thing that most frequently results in a future stock.

Here was a top management and design team that had left a superb high-technology company to form one on its own that would produce a brilliantly conceived new product with vast market potential.

There were a number of aspects to the Prime concept. First, Prime took advantage of sliding prices for electronic components in designing an advanced minicomputer others didn't think to make because the parts had been too expensive.

Further, Prime designed in a universal software package, adaptable to any new hardware the company developed, and thus avoided major future costs experienced by most other computer makers. Prime came up with a superb package offering mainframe capacity at minicomputer prices.

Prime had previously determined that the potential market for its equipment was large enough to provide exceptional growth, even assuming that aggressive rivals eventually entered the market. What's more, the company recognized that prudent use of borrowed capital could multiply returns on invested capital and didn't hesitate to employ it.

Management and concept both impressed Wall Street, and by 1975 Prime was selling at 27 times earnings. But by 1977, when sales reached $50 million, a degree of disenchantment had set in and the P/E had dropped to 12.

In that year, Prime's return on equity at 24.7 percent wasn't too different from IBM's 21.6 percent. (In the *Value Line Investment Survey* return on equity is styled, "% earned net worth.")

But thereafter, an astonishing thing happened. Prime's return on equity rose to 33 percent in 1978 as the company began to grow rapidly, and ROE reached an amazing 38 percent in 1979. Meantime, sales nearly doubled, to reach $93.6 million in 1978. Sales leaped to $152 million in 1979 and $268 million in 1980.

Not just incidentally, this growth was financed in part by leverage. In June, 1978, Prime borrowed $20 million through 6¾ percent 20-year convertible debentures—high-technology's best money friend.

The result of this debt-financed growth: By 1980, Prime's book value per share was up almost 2,000 percent, while IBM's rose a mere 50 percent or so.

Everyman's Bottom Line: Bounding Share Price Appreciation

Prime's share price results were even more impressive. Remember that by the usual Wall Street test—the price-earnings ratio—Prime shares seemed abundantly priced before all this happened. In 1975, Prime sold at 27 times earnings, which seemed an especially rich valuation in a year when the stock market generally was off. In short, Prime looked to be an incredibly risky situation.

A $10,000 Investment in Prime in 1975 Was Worth $800,000 by 1981

But by the end of 1980, Prime shares had reached $40 relative to a price (adjusted for prior splits) of 50 cents a share in 1975. That's an 80-fold gain in a five-year time span.

By contrast, assuming the investor bought IBM at the low of 39 in 1975, his best gain would have been to 73 in 1980. The shares did not even double in value. A $10,000 investment in IBM in 1975 was worth less than $20,000 by 1981.

The point is that most investors were unwilling to pay enough for Prime Computer, a true growth situation. Prime, unlike so many other high-technology companies with excellent prospects, recognizes the importance of high return on equity and follows policies designed to produce a high return—including the leverage that comes from borrowing money. By contrast, Hewlett-Packard, for example, is more interested in remaining as debt-free as possible, and its long term debt of $29 million represents just 2 percent of capital. Partly as a result, the company has not grown enough to qualify for future stock status.

CAVEAT: *Anyone considering Prime shares should be aware that Kenneth Fisher, the popular and highly innovative chief executive, left in mid-1981 following an extended dispute with the chairman over Prime's future direction. Prime will continue to prosper, no doubt, but growth may be substantially reduced.*

Winning Combo: High ROE Plus Rising Book

Look for return on equity in excess of 20 percent as a good measure of a company's ability to employ capital. What's more, a dip in return on equity can be an early sell signal. But ROE isn't the whole story. If book value per share growth is lagging, the company is in trouble.

To obtain a forecast of book value per share, divide common shares outstanding into estimated total earnings per share. Subtract the dividend, if any, and you will see how much will be added to book value per share in that year. It is hard to do a similar analysis of return on equity, but the trend should be obvious. (See table on page 177 for detailed methodology.)

Item: Data Terminal Systems, which produces electronic cash registers and point-of-sale terminals, experienced disappointing market growth so that its debt, amounting to 38 percent of equity, taxed earnings in a period of record high interest rates.

The company then did something that would appall sophisticated investors in high-tech shares. Though Data Terminal's return on equity peaked in 1977, the company chose that year to begin paying dividends.

ROE reached 47.1 percent in 1977, dropped to 38.6 percent in 1978—a year in which the company began to experience a decline in ROE in real terms—and plummeted to 21.2 percent in 1979.

But additions to book value would clearly slow as a result of the dividends begun in 1977 and increased in subsequent years. To Mitchell and Company, falling return on equity taken with the payment of a dividend constituted a clear sell signal.

Anyone using the Mitchell method would have bailed out of Data Terminal in 1978, for the company peaked before the shares soured. The shares made an all-time high in 1978 at 50. Even so, institutional investors didn't begin earnest selling of Data Terminal until 1980, when the shares began a drop that would soon take them down to 15.

Main point: Unless book value per share is rising at a rate of 26 percent a year after inflation and return on equity is higher than 20 percent and holding relative to inflation, marked share gains are unlikely. The shares of any such company are eventually going to experience selling pressure. Don't wait for the avalanche.

What to look for:

1. Some companies pursue policies that tend to grow book value per share faster than others and such growth goes hand in glove with share price appreciation.

2. Companies that are growing at very rapid rates usually issue new equity or convertible debentures to pay for this growth. Within reason this is good, even essential.

3. Dividends make no sense for high-tech companies, which, if successful, will be using up capital faster than they can generate it. Besides, dividends trim additions to book value per share.

4. Inflation will be taken care of almost as a matter of course in a superior high-tech company. Well-run high-tech companies with superior management and product grow faster than inflation. When inflation was 1 to 3 percent in the 1960s, well-run high-tech companies such as Digital Equipment Company sustained earnings growth of at least 40 percent a year. In the hyperinflation of today, the best high techs will sustain 50 percent growth or more.

5. (A corollary to 4.) Except for an extremely large company like IBM, a company with growth of 20 percent or less a year is either not very good at technical innovation or its market is mature. What's more, if the stock market has a couple of bad years, the shares of companies with that kind of growth will

> drop and won't come back for years. A faster-growing company can bounce back after a bear market in six months.

Building for the Future: Those Critical First-Time Buyers

The prospects of a high-tech company in a large new market will be determined by its *continuing ability* to secure first-time users as customers, for a high-tech company cannot thrive on repeat business alone.

Thus, it is critical that a high-tech company land a significant number of the first-time users each year. Moreover, its share of the first-time user market must remain constant or grow if the company is to excel.

Warning: If your company's share of first-time users is down in a given year, it is time to think about getting out.

In fact, when a company's share of first-time users starts to come down, it is almost invariably fatal to the company's hopes of remaining an important factor in the market. When this happens, the company has undoubtedly made a big mistake somewhere. By the time the company's absolute share of market begins to drop, it is already too late for shareholders to take cover. The selling will have begun in earnest.

The Other Side of the Coin: Why Repeat Business Is Important

Obviously business comes from repeat customers as well as from first-time users. Remember the loyalty of the high-tech customer who cannot afford to change systems. This business is beneficial for the manufacturer because the repeat business costs less to book. But without securing the new business, the manufacturer obviously misses out on the repeat business.

How do you find out what part of a company's sales revenues represent first-time users? Call the company. The individual who handles investor relations will be eager to tell you—if the company is doing well. Once you know the company's first-time user sales, you will need to know what the rest of the industry is doing to determine whether the company is actually holding share of market. Again, ask the investor relations person.

Better still, visit a business library and look at *Datapro Reports.* This sophisticated publication gives detailed breakdowns of sales by individual companies and even discusses the level of customer satisfaction.

Datapro figures are detailed enough so that you can estimate your company's share of market and its share of the first-time user market. You will be able to tell which companies are experiencing growth in market share and which are lagging. You will also learn how rapidly the market is growing and the apparent limits of that market.

SUMMARY: *Buy shares at outrageous multiples if appropriate, but recognize that you are taking a risk—even when the company has a lock on an important market. Remember to buy on weakness, and you might glance at the high-low theory of buying stocks for further grounding in that approach. The last generation of high-tech stocks—including IBM, Xerox, and the like—advanced over a period of at least 20 years, and gains of a select group of such issues amounted to 75 times compared with four times for the market generally. Thus an investment of $20,000 would have been worth $80,000 if invested in the averages and $1,500,000 if invested in the high-tech group. Interim sinking spells didn't hurt the long-term holder.*

9

Some Additional Buy Strategies

When to Buy Them

CONCEPT: *Chart past performance of your future stock candidates for their characteristic market patterns. Buy them near their years' lows for early market gains. You'll need several holdings for an element of stability and a shot at more than one big winner.*

Samuel C. Greenfield has made a career out of the study of stock fluctuations. His Low-High Theory of Investment *became a book published by Coward McCann, Inc. (New York) in 1968.*

The Low-High Theory of Investment

Greenfield notes that stocks reach a low and a high point each year. Obviously, if you can buy shares when they are at a low ebb and sell them when they are high, you've got to make money—as long as the swing is more than wide enough to compensate the broker. Even with today's hefty commissions, the spread in the volatile future stocks has got to be that wide. In fact, in such stocks the difference between the low and the high in a single year may be as much as 100 percent. By contrast, American Telephone & Telegraph usually makes a spread of just 25 percent.

Greenfield would buy AT&T at what appeared to be the low in

terms of its past market performance and sell it at the apparent high—when the spread had been made. He would buy it again when the spread appeared to have been made on the next downside.

By contrast, investors in future stocks should buy for long-term performance and would thus hold shares purchased at the lower end of the yearly price scale and perhaps buy more on the next downswing—thereby adding to portfolio holdings.

The best time to catch the average stock near its low is just after the end of the year. December, as you know, is the last month for investors to sell stocks and establish tax losses. But, on the other hand, some stocks sell at or near their highs for the year in December. Future stocks often sell at high levels in December. If your favorite growth stock is at a high in December, don't buy it then. You will succeed much more rapidly if you buy at or near the year's low.

Let's assume that a growth stock does set a low in December. Chances are that if you buy then you will be ahead of the game quickly—perhaps in four or five months.

Back to the Drawing Board

Do an analysis of the prior lows and highs. That will give you an idea of what the stock will do in the current year—no guarantee, but a pretty good idea of direction, assuming the fundamentals hold up. Fundamental analysis is, of course, an important part of the exercise. If there are signs that suggest unequivocally that the high-growth game is over in a particular stock, then you won't want to continue your buying program.

Greenfield looked at several companies mentioned at length in this book—Cray Research, Intel Corp., Tandem Corp., Texas Instruments, and Wang.

In rapidly growing Cray Research, the pattern is interesting. In 1976, the spread from low to high was a mere 58 percent. But in the next year the spread reached 100 percent, and the year after that, 224 percent. The trend of highs is emphatically upward from year to year, yet the shares fluctuate enough on the down side to carry the shares well below the new high-water mark set in the following year.

Some Additional Buy Strategies

Intel Corporation also shows violent price spreads from year to year. Once again, the low of each year is significantly lower than the high of the preceding year.

Tandem, also a young company, shows a characteristic growth-company pattern. Its lows each year are higher than the lows of the preceding year. The spreads characteristically are over 100 percent.

The more mature growth company, Texas Instruments, offers a different picture. When the prices are low, the swings are large, and when the prices are high, they are modest. It is important to note that the low of a succeeding year is significantly lower than the high of the previous year. Millions have been made in Texas Instruments. But millions have been lost by those who bought at or near the highs.

Wang Lab shares have varied significantly, with spreads normally in the 100 to 200 percent range. While shares of Wang and other companies mentioned here can tumble, it is still reasonable to expect that the spread over the year will be in the 100 percent range.

This then is the technique employed in the low-high theory of investing. Master it, and your gains are likely to materialize faster—even in future stocks.

Fisher of Stocks

The young fisherman was after the biggest fish ever seen in the lagoon, a giant black grouper. Grouper meat is popular in the Caribbean, but the fisherman had no intention of selling the fish for food. He wanted it for a nearby aquarium that had offered $1,000 to anyone delivering the giant grouper live.

But the fish the young man was after was as elusive as the Loch Ness monster. Though some claimed to have seen a giant grouper prowling the waters of the lagoon, cynics chuckled when a wag commented that the fish was a tropical cocktail squeezed out of rum, rock, shadow, and a splash of imagination.

Still, the young fisherman kept casting—though he often spent hours dislodging his hook from dark stones that resembled a slow-moving grouper in the shimmering waters of the lagoon.

Once in a misty predawn, he was hip-deep in the water when a large fish or turtle brushed against his leg. But apart from that, the young fisherman had never glimpsed anything large enough to be his prey.

One day as he cast from the shore, an old fisherman stood nearby, pulling fish out of the water with a net. After one particularly good pass, the older man picked several small fish out of the net, gutted them expertly with a knife, and popped them into a frying pan suspended over a beach fire. The young fisherman spoke with more sarcasm than he had intended in saying, "You'll never land The Big One with that equipment. I fish with a heavy line—if I ever hook that big grouper, I'll surely land him."

"If you find him," the old man said mildly, adding, "Oh, you're right to use a hook for your quarry, of course," as he forked small fry out of the pan and popped them into his mouth. It was chilly and the young man was hungry. He watched in famished silence, wondering if his brashness had cost him an invitation to breakfast.

The successful fisherman nodded in the direction of a couple of groupers idling in the water, nylon string threaded through their gills: "I put my best groupers in a secret ocean enclosure. One of them may grow enough to interest the aquarium in time. Anyhow, most of them will survive and some will be quite big some day. I'll make a profit when I sell them on the market—even if I don't have a world champion."

Love Somebody—But Never Love a Stock

Similarly, many investors spend their time searching for the one big stock of the future and never get around to filling a portfolio. Those who limit their investment to a single stock surely miss many fine opportunities and may even lose most of their capital on a loser.

A professional money manager in Philadelphia followed a policy roughly like that, investing in one stock at a time. He would pick out the single stock he felt most likely to double in value over a few months time—usually because the company was a takeover candidate. He would then put every dollar he could lay his hands on into that single situation. It was like a parlay at a race track: bet heavily on one horse, and, winning, put all the proceeds on the next horse, and so on. It was difficult and risky. Nevertheless, this highly qualified professional man-

Some Additional Buy Strategies

aged to build his small stake into a low six-figure fortune in a few years.

However, his investment choice at the time I wrote about him in my Market Place column became a minor disaster. The shares were trading at a level several points below his average cost at press time. Fully invested in this one stock, this thoughtful and intelligent investor would have reduced his entire capital pool substantially had he not sensed trouble in time to bail out, something less knowledgeable investors are rarely able to do.

Let George Do It

George J. Stasen, an experienced money manager who runs Medical Technology Fund, Inc., has focused his search for future stocks in medicine, where he believes a subrevolution paralleling the high-technology revolution is underway. He carries a big net, holding scores of fast-growing medical stocks, not just a couple of situations that appear to be highly promising.

He notes that one could have participated in the computer revolution of the 1950s and 1960s with Sperry, the inventor of the mainframe computer, RCA, a major innovator in the field, and General Electric, one of the best-run companies of all time. The investor with those shares in his portfolio probably chalked up small gains, but nothing worth writing about. You had to own IBM or Control Data to make it big.

Speaking in terms that inspired the opening paragraphs of this chapter, Mr. Stasen comments:

> My role is like that of the experienced fisherman. For so large a catch, I want a net, not a fishing pole. My challenge is to construct and manage a portfolio which will capture the major opportunities this revolution will create. As the Fund's assets continue to grow, I expect to increase diversification and will probably hold shares in more than 70 companies.
>
> One has to concentrate on working and deploying a portfolio net, rather than looking for another IBM. I made that mistake too often years ago and hope that I am profiting from the experience.

As individuals we can concentrate, or we can diversify. Unless we choose to invest in, say, a well-run mutual fund like the Oppenheimer

Special Fund, Eberstadt's Surveyor, or George Stasen's Medical Technology Fund, to cite examples of funds seeking appreciation through emerging stocks, we cannot buy scores of stocks for our portfolios. We'd have to be rich to begin with to do that.

The author believes that there is a happy medium for small investors—a portfolio concentrating on several situations with some overlap. For example, the investor might buy the shares of one microprocessor manufacturer; one CAD/CAM company; and one tagalong company that makes a product every company in a large, high-technology industry must use. He might add a larger high-tech company like DEC with future stock promise to give some stability to a portfolio that is likely to be volatile. Even though you are buying for long-term profits, those market dips can be frightening.

Be careful not to buy too many stocks. An individual's personally managed portfolio probably shouldn't contain a dozen stocks. To steal a title from television, "Eight Is Enough." Unless you do nothing else, you won't be able to follow more than a handful of companies, and it will take some doing just to learn enough about a few companies to justify an investment. Strike a happy medium. Take the advice of an old pro, George Stasen. Use a net, not a fishing pole. You won't go hungry and you may very well get rich.

SUMMARY: *Once you've singled out your future stock candidates, remember the basic rule for buying anything. Buy cheap. Chart your stocks and buy them at their years' lows. Don't buy too many stocks, but buy enough for a shot at success. If four $10,000 mid-1970s investments went no place in particular and the fifth was Prime Computer, you'd still be rich.*

10

Bailing Out: How Broad the Pond? How High the Moon?

CONCEPT: *Rapidly growing markets mature—often when enthusiasm is highest. But you can anticipate market maturity in plenty of time to protect your hard-won gains in future stocks.*

Future stocks draw us like a romantic opera that ultimately ends in tragedy. The pulsating swing to the upper register fills us with joy. But over time, the beautiful music eventually takes on ominous overtones. The shares that soared so magnificently must settle to earth. Yet the orchestra plays on sonorously, promising more, beckoning us still. At some point, we're never sure just when, the music begins to signal danger. We must never forget that a stock market odyssey—like the opera—can end tragically. As investors we must protect ourselves against this eventuality. We must leave the house before the finale—before the death knell is sounded.

We all know that markets, however large, inevitably are exploited to such a degree that growth must slow. Great companies—and great industries—eventually saturate markets.

But it isn't always possible to know a company's sales potential. When IBM had sales of a billion dollars, it was still an infant. On the other hand, a hula hoop manufacturer may experience a mature market before sales top $100 million. Since, both companies—IBM and the hula hoop maker—must eventually meet their marketing Waterloo, the investor must be eternally vigilant. Stocks decline just as people do; the investor must not stay for the wake, as he may lose his legacy.

In order to gauge the degree to which a company has saturated its markets, the investor will find it necessary to evaluate the economy and individual earnings reports with cold impartiality. This calls for a kind of negative thinking to which investors, great believers in the future, are unaccustomed.

Your negative thinking must be done at a time when market enthusiasm is at a peak—when everyone is exuberant about future prospects. At such times, contrary thinking is essential.

By analogy it may be useful to think about the problem in terms of one town's approach to eliminating a potentially threatening local attraction.

Padtime for Bonzo

There was a large pond in a bedroom community near the city. The neighborhood teenagers loved to bathe there, preferring its spring-fed freshness to the chlorined waters of the local swimming pool. But the pond was not safe. Deep and quite cold in spots, it was threatening to inexperienced swimmers who ventured out too far and to stronger ones who liked to eat and swim by turns. More to the point, there were no lifeguards.

Parents worried that one of the younger children might enter the water unobserved, swim out, grow weary, and sink beneath the surface to drown. One of the town fathers, a man with a knowledge of horticulture, came to the next meeting with a plan. Water lilies, he said, would soon discourage all swimming. "Buy one, get one free," he quipped. For he knew that these aquatic plants multiply extremely rapidly. The man, like so many who tend flowers for pleasure, was basically shy. But standing before his fellow townsmen, he began to enjoy their attention. He cleared his throat and stated emphatically that his lilies would soon cover the entire pond.

Smiling now, he spoke deliberately and with some confidence, tapping the conference table lightly with a forefinger for emphasis. He insisted that a single lily planted in mid-pond could do the job forthwith.

By the second day, he said, the first lily would be joined by a second. On day three the lily population would double to four. On day four the population would double again to eight lilies. He said that he had visited the pond to determine its girth. With that, he drew a battered envelope from his jacket pocket. He looked at the calculations he had scribbled on the back. Ticking off the figures, he told his peers that the geometric progression by which lilies multiply would populate the pond in exactly 30 days. But several days before that, the action would be noticeably swift. To wit, on the penultimate, or 29th, day, the pond would only be half full and the children would still be able to swim with some freedom.

Thoroughly enjoying himself now, the horticulturist hooked his thumbs in his vest pockets after the manner of Clarence Darrow, and concluded expansively, "Imagine our children's surprise on day 30. The party will be over. The kids will admire the lilies and troop to the municipal swimming pool. Ed Smith's toy poodle, Bonzo, will be able to prance across the lilypads without wetting his paws." With that the horticulturist bowed pompously to weak smiles from the crowd and returned to his seat, grinning like a dolphin eating chum.

Sure enough, what the lily expert said would happen did in fact come to pass. The "old swimming hole" has become "the lily pond," and no one goes there these days except, maybe, Bonzo.

Wringing the Market Dry

And so it is with rapidly growing companies in rapidly growing industries. Using the lily analogy to mirror growth companies that fill marketing "ponds," investors need to know when the pond is half-full since the action thereafter is breathlessly swift. The companies serving the market continue to grow until, almost overnight, it seems, the market is saturated. Our problem as investors in future stocks is twofold. Obviously we must find the stocks that grow more rapidly than the rest in the first instance, and then we must be sure to sell them before the game is over. If we've chosen well, this may not occur for years—perhaps decades. But ultimately it will happen and sell we must. When to sell is, as Wall Streeters freely admit, the most difficult decision of all and may be the most critical. For when the marketing pond is nearly full, the stock market pond will be too.

Premiums for Slow Growth

To emphasize, investors often continue to pay a premium for growth after the limits of that growth should be obvious and even, in some cases, after growth has in fact slowed. When the price-earnings multiple has become bloated, it is no wonder the market reaction is fierce as the awful truth becomes apparent.

Worse yet, some heavily laden institution is likely to see the situation in true perspective first and, as the end draws near, clobber the market with a sale in some multiple of 100,000 shares. A price reaction that might have occurred over a period of weeks in the old days when individual investors dominated the market and sold shares in 200- and 300-share lots occurs instead in a twinkling.

Disaster and Greed, Its Handmaiden

Greed is the handmaiden of disaster. As human beings and investors, we must protect ourselves against it. Greed can make us look as ridiculous as the precocious but demented collegian the author knew who wore two bow ties. "Why?" asked the author. Demented scholar: "Well . . . you wear one bow tie and you look good, right? I wear two, and I look twice as good." Thus, impeccable logic can lead to a ludicrous conclusion. But investors expecting to double their money again and again follow a strangely similar course, knotting new Wall Street ties when it's time to get undressed and go to bed.

There's another helpful Wall Street expression illustrating the point. "There are three kinds of animals in Wall Street—bulls, bears, and pigs. Bulls and bears make money—pigs never do." How do we distinguish greed from sound analysis of fundamentals?

Question: When 15 Beats 100

Let's forget the young company that manages to double sales for a time. As we've implied, sell a single widget in year one and it won't be difficult to sell two in the second year and four in the third year and so on. But sell a million items in one year and you've got your work cut out for year two if you plan to double sales. Small, low-base young companies don't sell a million units as a rule, and, besides, they are highly risky enterprises suitable for venture capitalists.

In order to get an appreciation of what it takes to sustain high growth, let's consider the problem of attaining growth somewhat below that which we are seeking in our quest for future stocks. Let's look at companies offering 15 percent growth.

Generally speaking, share price tends to go up at about the same rate as sales and earnings, assuming that book value per share is growing at about the same rate while return on equity is holding relative to inflation. Since the market places a premium on its growth, share price of the superior company will grow even faster than sales and earnings. But consider how difficult it is to maintain a growth of 15 percent and see why so few companies do so.

Investors tend to forget what that rate of growth does to all but the most sizable markets.

Growth Ad Infinitum?

Ergo, assume that a small high-technology company shipped 1,000 mainframe computers last year. A 15 percent unit growth does not mean selling 150 mainframes, of course; rather, the company would have to ship 1,150 mainframes in the second year—the company will have to identify a need and sell computers to serve 1,150 new applications for old and new customers or influence old customers with 1,150 old computers to replace them with new ones. Any mix of the above will work, but obviously it isn't all that easy. Ask any computer salesman. Or ask your Fuller Brush man how hard it is to produce sales that grow half that fast year after year.

Let's say, for the sake of argument, that the total market for these particular mainframes is 20,000. If the company ships 1,000 mainframes in the first year and keeps shipping at that rate, it will take 20 years to saturate the market—barring ever-present competition, of course. But 15 percent growth compounded annually calls for sales of 1,150 mainframes in the second year, as we have seen. That growth rate calls for 1,323 mainframe sales in the third, 1,521 in the fourth, 1,749 in the fifth, and 2,012 in the sixth year. On that basis, saturation would occur in just 13 years—again assuming no competition, and stable prices. Remember that price cuts are common in many high-tech products and this, too, can be a major drag on revenue, as investors in some of the high-tech companies have discovered.

Let's hypothesize plant efficiency as a constant, with no price cuts. Sales and earnings would move up more or less in lockstep. So 15 percent growth in unit sales in this example would be synonymous with 15 percent growth generally. Accomplish this, and share price should move up at least as fast so long as the future continues bright and market saturation doesn't occur. But some time short of 13 years, it would become clear that this particular lily pond was filling up. Unless the company developed new products with different markets, the growth would be over and the shares would come down.

World Champion Chicken Plucker

Let's look at an example of what extremely high growth demands of the entrepreneur. In the late 1960s, Minnie Pearl Chicken franchises were being authorized at a rate that doubled every quarter. That obviously couldn't last. The company's chief executive, John Jay Hooker, had tied his business aspirations to his political aspirations. Though an unsuccessful candidate for governor of a Southern state, he still hoped someday to become president.

But as each quarter loomed, and he strained to double sales, he began to complain that he felt like a man on a tiger. Obviously he had an impossible task. Even so, the growth claims were misleading because Mr. Hooker was allocating to profits some large franchise fees from the sales of regional franchises even though few stores were open-

Bailing Out: How Broad the Pond? How High the Moon?

ing and despite the fact that some of the fees were paid by former associates who "purchased" regional franchises with IOUs.

Even if the scores of stores had in fact opened, sooner or later it would have taken more chicken franchises than the nation's chicken-breeding capacity would sustain to maintain the rate of growth Hooker aspired to. This may seem obvious, but speculators who bought shares in that company didn't notice, and they seemed to include some Wall Street "smart money" operators. Presumably, the pros expected to bail out early enough to realize their paper profits. But when the deluge came, it roared into the valley like a rain-swollen stream. Almost no one was nimble enough to make money on that turkey.

Minnie Pearl, also known as Performance Systems, illustrates why individuals who seek rapid growth must pick carefully. The message here: Buy high technology and avoid fowl play. You can't afford to gamble on speculative shares reflecting unrealistic estimates of a market's girth.

IBM: The Exceptional Case?

Let's look at a solid situation for an insight into growth prospects in a market that, on its face, appears to be overfull. It's time for another look at the market for the nation's premier high-technology company. Examine the potential for IBM—which seems to be a has-been by the tests of this book. Whereas a market potential of, say, $250 million might be excessive for a small specialty computer company, $25 billion in world revenues may not preclude substantial growth for IBM in the years ahead. At least, IBM may experience sufficient growth to make it a solid holding in a portfolio of somewhat more volatile future stocks.

The reason IBM could just experience growth at the requisite 15 percent compounded to make it a born-again growth company is that IBM stands astride the computer market like a Colossus. Thus, IBM could well produce better than 15 percent growth for some time to come, and there are those in Wall Street who are betting that this will happen. It would be a welcome change after nearly a decade of marking time.

The argument for IBM assumes the market for all computer makers, software companies, and so forth will eventually account for several times the 2 percent of GNP they account for now. Some believe computers and allied equipment and software will someday account for 10 percent of gross national product. Here's the argument: As recently as the 1950s, the automobile industry accounted for 23 to 25 percent of gross national product. Obviously this figure includes sales of dealers, original equipment producers, gas stations, and repair shops. Even so, GM experienced a period of unusually rapid growth as this degree of economic concentration in auto-allied industries was occurring. Question: Isn't it possible that computers may become just as important to the economy as automobiles did in years past?

IBM: New Directions

Here's another point: IBM's world sales account for 1 percent of the $2.5 trillion national economy, but IBM's domestic revenues were only $11 billion out of a total of $26 billion in 1979.

IBM's biggest chance for renewed growth is regarded by some analysts as in the field of generalized intercompany "networking," or distributed data processing. An analyst explains:

> Networking is not just data bases—pages of numbers—but "relational" software. Relational software will make networking possible. There is a huge market for networks. If a computer memory bank can be set up to handle difficult queries, that's something. The customer might want to know where he can buy Comet cleanser at the cheapest possible wholesale price. The software would have to handle that in plain English and relate it to what you need. In this case the relation is to price. Present programs show two separate numbers—one identifying the product and a different one identifying the price. What is needed is a network program that will go through the data and sort out all the different prices so that the logic step "cheapest" can be completed.

What IBM is doing is developing the software for use with the data bases everyone is building. The real problem is to offer the data base in usable form—to myriad customers. This work appears to offer the most promise for IBM's resurgence.

Break Up IBM!

There are those who fervently hope that the Justice Department will prevail and that IBM will be broken up into a number of pieces. And there are a few savvy professional investors who predict this will happen. The result for investors could be a number of small superbly managed high-technology companies and a handful of future stock candidates with few peers in the world. Don't bank money on this development, but be prepared to act quickly if it happens.

Selling: The Lesson of History

As any seasoned investor knows, the fastest-growing companies often face the peril of an institutional bail-out. In the early 1970s—the end of the last previous era of high-growth companies—growth shares resisted for many months the ferocious bear market that began in 1969. It was happenstance that many of these companies were rounding out the periods of their greatest growth at that time.

The End of a Golden Era

The end was traumatic in the extreme—and a long time coming. The groundwork for the last hurrah of the Favorite Fifty was laid in the frothy bull market of the late 1960s. By 1970, some sober observers were beginning to sense that disaster was on the way. They concluded that the shares of most of these exciting companies had reached levels far higher than the shares would have traded given a rational interpretation of future prospects.

Naturally, the institutions were loathe to terminate so wondrous an era. But when a child's balloon springs a leak, however small, it eventually goes down. The debacle for the Favorite Fifty actually began in the mid-1970s—long after most previously popular shares had spiraled downward. The slide of the conglomerators and the fast-food companies in the early 1970s signaled the end of the major bull market of the 1960s.

Thereafter, the supergrowth stocks had become a refuge in the memorialized market environment. But the survivors were held to impossible standards. A single disappointing quarter for a supergrowth stock brought on huge selling as institutional investors raced each other to the telephone. It was panic by the numbers, with each week bringing a new superstock disappointment and another sell-off.

Accounting tricks helped a few corporations maintain the fiction of extraordinary growth in some instances, but finally all cherished stocks were exposed to the hard light of reality. Institutions were relearning a fundamental lesson. Supergrowth simply is not sustainable forever. One by one, the stock market Vestal Virgins, as they were also known, began falling out of bed.

Of the great companies, Polaroid, fell the hardest. In 1973, shares of this Cambridge-based manufacturer of picture-in-a-minute cameras—a superachiever among high-tech companies as among stock market performers—reached 149½. But Polaroid's earnings growth, always erratic, became a problem again, and less than a year later, the shares had plummeted all the way to 14⅛ as institutions threw Polaroid shares at their brokers 100,000 at a time.

Polaroid was a spectacular example in the biggest market crash since the great one of 1929. And the stock market debacle of the 1970s, like that of 1929, ended one of the greatest eras in stock market history. It was sobering for everyone. During this bear market period, most mutual funds and bank trust departments lost 25 to 50 percent of their owners' and clients' money. Individuals lost at least as much. No one had seen anything like it in over 35 years.

How then does one avoid this? It isn't easy. But if you are to increase your capital tenfold, you must be prepared to sell treasured shares when the play is over.

SUMMARY: *Never lose sight of the fact that both markets and individual companies mature. Make a determined effort to discover the size of the lily pond by asking questions of management and by reading trade publications in a good business library. Be sure there is still enough room in the marketing pond for rapid growth and make sure your company is holding its own—particularly in terms of sales*

Bailing Out: How Broad the Pond? How High the Moon?

to first-time users. (See the chapter on outrageous multiples.)

In short: You not only have to gauge market saturation factors but also your company's continuing ability to compete in markets that are still burgeoning.

Remember that unless your company's book value per share is rising and return on equity is larger than 20 percent and/or rising further share gains are unlikely (see page 169).

Remember also that once revenue and earnings growth sinks to 20 percent or less, there are added negatives. That rate of growth simply is not enough in inflationary times. Besides, as we have seen, that rate of growth marks a company that either isn't very good at technical innovation or one whose market is maturing. One critical consequence: Shares of faster-growing companies will snap back after a bear market; those of the slower-growing companies will not. Further share gains are unlikely. It's time to find a new future stock.

11

Stock Futures: 27 Potential Winners

Now that you understand the main concept of future stocks, let's consider some stock futures—companies to watch that could provide the tenfold gains we seek.

These stocks are thought to be at least that promising by one or more of the author's Wall Street contacts. Do not misunderstand. These are not buy recommendations—but ideas for you to explore in the context of the stock market, the economy, and the company's own prospects. That is, you'll have to apply the tests in this book to discover whether they are likely to work out.

A further caution: Since circumstances change frequently, the author suggests that the reader keep up to date by consulting the *Value Line Investment Survey* and/or Standard & Poor's Stock Reports for updates on key numbers and ratios discussed in this book.

You must, of course, evaluate fundamental factors, watching the newspapers for signs of slowing growth and/or growing pains. And, among other things, watch for major management defections, which can be a critical development. On the other hand, if an entire design team leaves a large, high-technology company in a body, you may be looking at the first step in the formation of a new high-tech company of promise.

Here, then, is a list of 27 companies with prospects for providing gains large enough to result in ten-for-one rewards over the next ten years.

Stock Futures: 27 Potential Winners   177

Your Rosetta Stone to Riches:
Silhouette of a High-Tech Company Whose Stock May Soar

Key Indicator of Rapid Stock-Price Growth	Direction	Super Company Example				
		'81	'82	'83	'84	'85
Book Value per Share	26% per year over inflation	1.0	1.5	2.4	3.6	5.4
Return on Equity	15% plus percent and rising by 5 points a year or more	15	21	28	33	39
Debt-to-Equity Ratio	Under .3 to 1	.3	.24	.15	.12	.11
Price-to-Book Ratio	Over 1 percent and rising by* 40% or more a year	1.2	1.7	2.5	3.8	6.0
Dividend	0–10% of net earns	0	0	0	0	0
Earnings Reinvested	High and/or rising**	(Not Applicable. All earnings reinvested)				
Earnings Growth	26% or higher***	2.0	2.8	4.1	6.0	9.0

　　*　Example: Year 1: Share price 20; book 20 for a P/B ratio of 1. Year 2: Price 32; book 22 for a P/B ratio of 1.45.
　**　Good sign that company employs capital well.
***　Super Company growth (figures in millions of dollars)
　　　Table in consultation with Mitchell & Co.

CAVEAT: *In stocks there is never a guarantee of success of any dimension.*

27 Stepping Stones to Success

1. *Alpha Industries.* Concept: Tagalong company. (Success follows on the heels of the overall high-tech trend.) The sophisticated microwave components business is growing at a 30 percent annual rate and Alpha is keeping up. Faster communications speed is possible through microwave transmission, and Alpha makes key devices in this field necessary for commercial applications via satellite and terrestrial stations, and for military applications used in electronic countermeasures. Alpha's growth at the current rate seems assured, says Stephen Mc-Gruder.

CAVEAT: *Market for these components is so attractive that rampant competition may develop.*

2. *Analog Devices.* Concept: Explosive growth in analog devices is the basis for this excellent company. All kinds of equipment must

deal with the real world—that of sound, light, temperature, pressure—at some point, and this is the province of Analog Devices. The company's niche is in high-performance, high-resolution analog circuitry necessary to do complicated jobs quickly and precisely. The company sets up ambitious five-year plans that more than meet our growth criteria, and so far it has surpassed its goals handily. Jim Magid notes that this has occurred even though the growth plans required constant infusion of both debt and equity capital. Analog Devices circumvented the hostile financial environment by selling equity at a substantial premium over market to Standard Oil of Indiana, thus insuring its ability to carry out its growth plans from financial strength. Sales were $135.7 million in 1980 and earnings per share were $1.40 on 6.7 million shares. In 1976, sales were $39.7 million and earnings per share were 41 cents.

CAVEAT: *In situations like this, something could go wrong. And, in fact, for two years things have been going wrong; also some combination of digital and analog circuits could take some of Analog Devices' market.*

3. *Applied Materials.* Concept: The best suppliers make better manufacturing equipment than semiconductor companies can make for themselves and are thus carving out a lucrative market. These suppliers will grow through two thrusts: as semiconductor companies turn to outsiders to an ever greater degree, and as the semiconductor market increases in size. Applied Materials is one of the larger semiconductor suppliers and represents a pure play. The company has an excellent past record, strong and broadening product line, and capable management. Not only have the highly competitive Japanese not discovered this market, they are customers for equipment, too.

CAVEAT: *When semiconductor manufacturers enter a cyclical slump, they cut back on equipment purchases. In last year's slump, Applied's backlog fell as did new orders, but not so hard as in the 1974–75 setback. Things have worsened since.(Otis Bradley.)*

Stock Futures: 27 Potential Winners

4. *Avantek.* Concept: Capitalizing on good luck: being in the right business at the right time. Avantek had expertise in both military and telecommunications when these markets began growing explosively. Sidelight: Emerson Electric balked at sweetening a purchase package for Avantek after its shares dropped relative to Avantek, then a private company. Since then—1977—Avantek's shares are up tenfold. Booming markets for microwave and satellite communications have caused this growth.

CAVEAT: *The company just happened to be in the businesses that grew rapidly and didn't have to seek them out. Avantek may not have the skill to perceive changes in the businesses it serves and protect its markets.*

5. *Aydin Corp.* Concept: A way to play the satellite market as more and more companies bypass telephone lines in exchanging information with distant offices. The company's high-power amplifiers and analog and digital communications equipment are used in satellite earth stations. The company also makes troposcatter terminals, which bounce microwave signals off the troposphere, and line-of-sight radios for medium- and short-range data transmission. The company maintains a balance between industrial and military customers. The company also provides computer terminals to electric utilities for monitoring power and has a line of rugged terminals for battlefield use. It builds high-power amplifiers and has been approached to build pulse modulators for fusion research, potentially a clean, abundant energy source. Long-term earnings growth, according to Value Line, is about 27.5 percent a year. In its record 1980 calendar year, Aydin sales advanced 76 percent while earnings were up about 70 percent.

CAVEAT: *Systems business is the main swing factor in any year's sales gain and Aydin didn't win major contracts in 1980. Backlog fell $22 million, to $115 million. The company is at the bottom end of the future stock range.*

6. *Computer Consoles.* Concept: Perpetual processing. High-capacity computers with redundant circuits that won't break down are produced for AT&T. With substantial software enhancement, the company hopes to sell to government and enter other commercial markets. Much earnings potential is built into Computer Consoles' conservatively stated lease base. Revenues increased 57 percent to $44 million in calendar 1980. Growth rate is anticipated at about 35 percent.

CAVEAT: *Prime product is reaching maturity and much depends on its success in addressing non-American telephone markets. AT&T buys centrally, making Computer Console's marketing easy relative to sales to other commercial customers.*

7. *Computervision* (see text).

8. *Cyclotron Corporation.* Concept: Growth arising out of heavy spending by foreign governments on nuclear medicine. The company is the world's leading maker of compact cyclotrons—nuclear particle accelerators. Since 1970 most of Cyclotron's sales have been to government-supported medical institutions in other nations, and, to a lesser extent, domestic and foreign commercial producers of radioisotopes. Cyclotrons and related equipment have accounted for 80 percent of volume for several years. A single order of this equipment can be of such magnitude that it will materially affect operating results for several years. In 1977 the company began development and manufacture of a compact high-performance neutron therapy system for use in treatment of human tumors resistant to other forms of radiation, a product which management believes has substantial potential. The company also produces a camera system for diagnosis of vascular and metabolic diseases and cancer and in the evaluation of treatment.

CAVEAT: *The company is still tiny, with sales of $10 million in 1980. Erratic earnings results reflect the fact that relatively few units are sold each year, but book value has been rising steadily, says George Stasen.*

9. *Datapoint* (see text).

Stock Futures: 27 Potential Winners

10. *Evans & Sutherland.* Concept: Little-noticed leader in some CAD applications. Leader in high-performance graphics and imaging systems used in flight simulation pilot training, computer-aided design, and scientific instruments. Mr. Sutherland is regarded as one of the creators of the concept of interactive computer graphics since his student days at MIT. In 1980, sales were $34.7 million and income was $2.27 a share, up from $4.8 million and 22 cents in 1975.

CAVEAT: *This is a highly competitive high-technology business with lots of new entrants. Expect uneven near-term results. Methods change rapidly, and to maintain leadership the company must be among the first to apply the new techniques as they develop, says Faith Griffin.*

11. *Flightsafety International.* Concept: Flightsafety is a tagalong company in which service considerations outweigh hardware. Pilots must be retrained throughout their careers, taking refresher courses required by Federal Aviation Administration. This was once done with actual flights with instructors monitoring the performance—occasionally with disastrous consequences. Flightsafety uses simulators with sophisticated displays, fast computers with lots of memory, and digital controls. Now the student "flies" a simulator and never leaves the ground. Perhaps $53 million in fuel has been saved by Flightsafety, but the company's courses cost only $49 million. Potential additional markets: pilot training for oil tankers and helicopters, both under development. Company is growing over 30 percent annually with good financial characteristics and no significant competition.

CAVEAT: *Corporations, a major market for Flightsafety, may depend more on commercial airlines in future instead of flying in self-owned planes. This would limit market potential. But reduction in air controller force has helped.*

12. *Floating Point Systems.* Concept: Piggyback "array processor" computers offer low-cost, high-speed number crunching capability. Array processors are, in effect, the minicomputers of the scientific computer market. By attaching an array processor to a host mainframe

computer or minicomputer, it is possible to do complicated mathematical calculations while at the same time utilizing the host computer for conventional data communications, file manipulations, and data acquisition routines. While sales were less than $10 million in 1977, they exceeded $40 million in the year ended October 31, 1980. John Westergaard expects 30 percent growth, so that by 1985 sales will reach $150 million and earnings $3.75 a share, the latter up from $1.02 in 1980.

CAVEAT: *Rapid growth often becomes unmanageable when a company approaches the critical $100 million sales level.*

13. *Flow General:* Concept: This high-technology drug company is typical of many companies of promise. It is small, and the risks of owning the shares are high. Flow General's main attractions are its team of superior researchers and the high-purity fibroblast interferon and human cells produced using patented methods. In making interferon, Flow General places human foreskin cells in a fermentation tank. The cells will only multiply when they adhere to the surface of the container. So Flow General introduces microscopic beads, called "superbeads," which offer vastly more surface area. A virus is then placed in the tank and the cells react as though under attack, producing interferon. The complete process takes ten days. Flow General's highly regarded purification methods were a factor in a production award by the National Cancer Institute. Flow General won the contract over such competitors as G. D. Searle and Abbott Laboratories. Flow General has been experimenting in another avant garde area for over 20 years—producing human cells from patient-donors for use in the treatment of the patients' own ailments, a process that also employs fermentation tanks and superbeads. Skin cells produced by this process are later joined together with collagen, an animal glue, to form human skin. Initial tests indicate that the body will not reject the tissue. The company plans to concentrate on the production of aorta tissue for use in circulatory disease. Prospects are unclear, but a formidable team of scientists is at work. Revenues, which totaled $42 million in fiscal 1977, reached $77.5 million in fiscal 1980, an overall gain of 84 percent. Correspondingly, net income from continuing operations advanced to an

Stock Futures: 27 Potential Winners 183

unusual degree—by a factorial 3.4 times, from $1.1 million in the base year to $3.8 million in fiscal 1980.

CAVEAT: *This company must be regarded as speculative, with few in Wall Street convinced that Flow General will succeed in bringing results of its novel medical research down to the bottom line. Watch its current low return on equity.*

14. *John Fluke.* Concept: Tagalong play. The company's test and measurement equipment is used in laboratories and in research, and increasingly in the manufacture of electronic products. The burgeoning market is for the repair, service, maintenance, and calibration of electronic products. With the revolution that the microprocessor is creating, every appliance, automobile, and word processor repairman will have to pack a digital multimeter—a simple tool in which Fluke leads. Further, a different new tool uses a microprocessor to analyze circuit boards containing microprocessors of their own, enabling a repairman to go immediately to the heart of any problem affecting this extremely complicated equipment. Jim Magid says that product could cut maintenance costs by hundreds of millions of dollars, as considerably less equipment will be sent back to the factory for repair. John Fluke revenues grew from $13.9 million in 1971 to $128.2 million in 1980 while earnings were rising from 13 cents to $1.56. Jim Magid expects comparable growth over the next decade.

CAVEAT: *At the low end of John Fluke's market there are a host of potential competitors. Meantime, the semiconductor slow-down has depressed growth.*

15. *Kevex Corp.* Concept: If you can't test it, you can't sell it; nondestructive, noninvasive materials testing in a manufacturing environment and in the oil field. Relatively inexperienced operators can achieve precise results in a manufacturing environment which a few years ago required PhDs working in a lab. Semiconductors and exotic materials require precision testing for quality and reliability. Kevex products are used in medical research, in the analysis of oil well samples, and in jet engine inspections, to name a few key uses. Sales were $1.7 million

in 1973, rose tenfold to $17 million in 1980, while net income per share grew from the equivalent of 5 cents a share in 1973 to 60 cents a share in 1980.

CAVEAT: *Can the company make the transition to a large one without stumbling?*

16. *KLA Instruments.* Concept: If you can't test it, you can't sell it. KLA manufactures automated electro-optical test systems which are used to inspect and evaluate photomasks used in the manufacture of large-scale integrated circuits (LSIs). The company's systems are sold to semiconductor manufacturers and to other manufacturers primarily in the computer telecommunications and automotive industries which manufacture LSI circuits for internal use. John Westergaard expects KLA to grow at a 75 percent annual rate for the next two years and at a 50 percent rate for two years after that; and at a 30 percent rate thereafter. Thus from a revenue base of $7.2 million for the fiscal year ended June 30, 1980, he projects revenues will reach $80 million by 1985 and earnings of $3.75 a share, up from 41 cents in fiscal 1980.

CAVEAT: *The company is still proving itself as an enterprise, and with such rapid growth it could falter. Further photomasks will become obsolete as electron beam technology emerges in ten years.*

17. *M/A-Com, Inc.* Concept: Getting into the soup-to-nuts data transfer and processing businesses through acquisitions. M/A-Com has moved from a small growth company to an important, medium-sized factor in the exploding data communications market. M/A-Com can process satellite signals at the dish level with its Prodlin acquisition; and behind the dish, with its Digital Communications and Linkabit acquisitions, it makes information usable over existing telephone or telegraph systems or through microwave transmission. The acquired Valtec division offers coaxial cable, and that division has fiber optics capability if coxial cable is later replaced. End terminals from Ohio-Scientific and Alanthus Data handle business and consumer applications. M/A-Com should be a major competitor in the distributed data communications and data processing markets in the 1980s and 1990s.

Stock Futures: 27 Potential Winners

CAVEAT: *The rapid pace of acquisitions could lead to indigestion. And M/A-Com must compete with telephone companies and newer entries such as Harris and Nippon Electronic. (Otis Bradley.)*

18. *MCI Communications.* Concept: An innovator in AT&T's $32 billion long-distance telephone market, now deregulated. The company is growing at a rate of 30 to 40 percent a year in this market. It is a relatively small company, serving a select portion of the market where telephones use is concentrated. Its capital equipment costs are lower than Ma Bell's because the equipment is more modern and operating costs are lower. Prices charged the customer are lower, and thus the appeal. MCI has experienced and should continue to experience current growth rates for perhaps two decades on a current revenue base of $150 million.

CAVEAT: *Regulation could return to cramp the company's growth. Also, capital costs are high in a period of soaring interest rates, says Stephen McGruder.*

19. *Paradyne.* Concept: "Modem" leadership coupled with exceptional management could provide long-term success. Modems convert computer-generated digital signals to a form suitable for transmission over the voice telephone system. This is the most rapidly growing company in Otis Bradley's high-technology universe. Revenue increased almost tenfold in the five years between 1975 and 1980—from $7.8 million to $75.9 million. Growth accelerated in 1980, up 83 percent from 60 percent. Long-term earnings per share could grow at a 55 percent a year rate, assuming appropriate equity financing. Exceptional management for such a small company, and offers a pure play. Social Security order for $84 million and possibly $150 million down the pike over next three to eight years was bigger than the company.

CAVEAT: *Paradyne competes with IBM and Ma Bell. Further, extraordinary growth could spin the wheels off. Management wheels could spin off, too, though Paradyne has excellent record in holding and attracting personnel.*

20. *Scientific-Atlanta.* Concept: Sensing the future and positioning a company to take advantage of it. Scientific-Atlanta is becoming a telling force in the merging technologies of satellite communication and cable television. Scientific's capability in satellite receivers is probably equal to the best. Cable TV is a recent line for Scientific but of increasing importance. Sidney Topol, the chief executive, heads a strong management team and is known for his vision regarding "macro" industry trends and his ability to position his company to take advantage of those trends. Growth at 35 percent is widely anticipated.

CAVEAT: *Scientific is yet to develop components capability in semiconductors and/or microwave components, which is critical for a full-line system competition in the data communications/distributed computing markets. (Otis Bradley.)*

21. *Scitex America Corporation.* Concept: Capitalizing on Israel's advanced research capability in graphics technology. Scitex makes computer-based color image processing systems for application in commercial color graphics reproduction as employed in the printing of magazines, catalogs, and advertising; in flexible packaging materials, maps, textiles, and wall and floor coverings. This is a large and important worldwide market, says John Westergaard, and one in which the company has a position of technological and marketing leadership. Scitex is expected to grow at an average annual compounded rate of 35 percent through 1985, which would take revenues that year to about $100 million versus $23 million in calendar 1980. Earnings could reach $2.50 a share in 1985, up from 71 cents in 1980.

CAVEAT: *The instability of the Middle East.*

22. *Spectra Physics.* Concept: The nation's supermarkets are rapidly converting to point-of-sale scanners for checkout counters and Spectra is a leader. The company's scientific instruments mostly end up in research labs. Recently lots of supermarkets have delayed installation of scanning systems and Spectra profits have slumped—40 per-

Stock Futures: 27 Potential Winners

cent in a recent quarter. Value Line says that Spectra knows how to turn research into profits—a key strength, particularly in lasers, where Spectra, a leader, is good at identifying potential uses and developing products to do the job.

CAVEAT: *Earnings growth, now projected at an anemic (for a future stock) 19.5 percent annual rate, could spurt with a more robust economy. Sales in 1980: $135 million. Delay this one at least until 1983.*

23. *Tandem Computer* (see text).

24. *United States Surgical Corp.* Concept: Twenty-first century surgical method. U.S. Surgical manufactures a unique line of surgical stapling instruments and disposable loading units for staples which have particularly impressed young doctors who are introduced to them in medical school. The range of products is broad, covering applications employed in both external and internal surgery, and the business has grown to substantial proportions even though probably no more than 20 percent of surgeons are using these products on a regular basis. Within 10 to 15 years the application should be pretty much universal as more and more surgeons using the old methods retire. For calendar 1980, revenues were $86 million, more than double the level of two years previously. John Westergaard anticipates that U.S. Surgical will grow at an average annual rate of 30 percent through 1985, taking revenues to $300 million and net earnings per share to $3.

CAVEAT: *Older surgeons will continue to use old-fashioned methods and in some cases may dictate hospital policy. Also, the company is approaching the difficult transition to large-company status, which usually occurs at the $100 million level. Possible "lilypad" problem here.*

25. *University Patents.* Concept: A pure royalty play in basic research. University Patents acts as broker between university and potential licensees. UPAT has right of first refusal on research emanating from ten universities, which spend a total of $500 million annually.

That sum represents about 2 percent of the basic research done by industrial America and equals almost $150 per UPAT share per year. The current royalty stream of $1 million should grow rapidly from existing projects. Several new projects in electronics, energy, batteries, and animal disease could contribute to significant profit improvement. Further, UPAT has access to extensive work in genetic engineering and may afford investors a bit of that action. Unlike most small speculative companies, financials are strong, with no long-term obligations, and the company's $9 million in government securities offers good liquidity. Growth in years ahead should be 30 percent. (Otis Bradley.)

CAVEAT: *UPAT has virtually no revenue (1 million in interest in addition to the $1 million in royalties) so that earnings are minimal at 15 to 20 cents a share in the current year.*

26. *Unimation.* Concept: Robotics play. Unimation is a world leader in the field, particularly in robots for automobile manufacture with over 4,000 units in place. The company's first public shares were about to reach the public market as this book went to press. Robotics is here to stay and may be one of the greatest growth industries of the twenty-first century.

CAVEAT: *The stock may well sell at fad price levels. Also, depressed conditions in the world auto market may depress sales on a short-term basis.*

27. *Wang B shares* (see text).

You will, of course, evaluate fundamental factors, watching the newspapers for signs of slowing growth and growing pains. And, among other things, watch for management defections, a critical variable. (On the other hand, if an entire design team leaves a large, high-technology company in a body, you may be looking at the first step in the formation of a new high-tech company of promise.)

12

The New Beginning

When Jerry Sanders speaks of the computer on a chip as the crude oil of the new industrial revolution, he is speaking about an industry—the semiconductor industry—that bills $8 billion today. But growth is so spectacular that semiconductors will account for $55 billion by the end of the decade and $100 billion by the end of this century. That's less than twenty years. Should this happen—and the author is confident that it will—the semiconductor companies will be huge, and the information industry gigantic.

Already, semiconductors fuel a $100 billion information industry. That is, Digital Equipment Corporation, Burroughs, and even IBM use the crude oil of semiconductors to build mini and mainframe computers, and their sales include a high-tech package of goodies for the alert investor. And that's only the beginning, as Jerry Sanders elaborates in his apt analogy.

The function of the computer makers is refining the crude oil. In turn, they send it through the pipeline to "the gas stations"—companies like Harris Corporation that do systems design work, some of it hardware, some of it software—so that as an end product (for Harris, for instance) type can be set without linotype machines. (The latter, a marvel in their time, are museum pieces today.) That is, Harris uses Digital Equipment minis—specifically, models 1134 and 1135 to store information in an elegant format that Harris' computer programmers have designed into the type-producing system.

Basically, the Harris system allows newspapers to use so-called "cold type" rather than hot lead. Reporters compose their stories sitting at computer terminals. After the copy is edited (also by terminal), it is set into type in the form of a photoengraving on a page formed on material that can be bent into a curve and buckled to a rotary press. (The photoengraving process is not new. Newspaper pictures have been produced by this process for a generation.)

The end result: Newspapers and other publishers operate more efficiently—the gas stations become more profitable, as it were. Other gas stations using the crude oil of semiconductors are information processors, who refine their retrieval techniques with the computer—recovering material lost in files since the beginning of their existence. In future, some information bank owners will become profitable enough to join the exclusive club of high-technology beneficiaries providing tenfold stock market gains in ten years.

In short, we are looking at a stunning array of vast markets, some known and some at present undeveloped, that will represent hundreds of billions of dollars in the foreseeable future. Future stocks will rise like nuggets in the pan. The savvy prospectors will pluck the stock market gold from the sand.

WITH THIS BOOK, YOU HAVE THE TOOLS TO CAPITALIZE ON THIS NEW SWEEP OF INDUSTRIAL HISTORY. AT THIS DAWNING OF THE MILLENNIUM, I PARAPHRASE THE PROPHET: GO FORTH AND MULTIPLY.

Index

Abbott Laboratories, 182
Addressograph, 93
Advanced Micro-Devices, 21, 46, 52, 60, 61, 62, 129
  cost reduction, 63
  debt, 64
  equity ownership, 64, 65, 67
  product, 62, 65, 66
Aftermarket, 48
Alanthus Data, 184
Alex Brown & Company, 97
Alpha Industries, 177
American Medical International, 2
American Stock Exchange, 52, 99
American Telephone and Telegraph Company, 84, 132, 142, 143, 144, 159, 180, 185
Analog Devices, 38, 177, 178
Analysts. *See* Security analysts
Annual reports, use of, 44
Apple Computer, 25, 145, 146, 147
Appliance Controls, 18
Applicon, 109, 110, 112
Applied Data Research, 99
Applied Materials, 178
Attached Resource Computer Software Architecture, 81, 82
Automatic Data Processing, Inc., 86, 90, 91, 94, 98, 103
Automatic Payrolls, Inc., 92
Auto-trol, 109, 110, 112
Avantek, 179
Avon Products, 29
Aydin Corporation, 179

BASIC programming language, 77
Batteries, 20, 123

Bendix, 25
Berdell, James R., 139
Berkeley, Alfred, 97, 98
Berkshire Hathaway, 34
Bonds, 5, 37
Book value, 132, 152, 155, 156, 169
Boston Corporation, The, 78, 79
Bowmar Brain, 74
Bowmar (Brain) Calculator Co., 80
Bradley, Otis, 185, 186, 188
Brean Murray, Foster Securities, Inc., 35
Browne, Malcolm W., 18
Bucy, Fred, 122
Buffett, Warren, 34, 35
Bureau of Labor Statistics, 115
Burroughs, 25, 189

CAD/CAM, 105, 117
  companies, 109, 110, 111, 112, 116
  defined, 106
  markets, 108, 109, 110, 111
  savings, 107
Calculator, 14, 15, 18, 57, 73, 74, 93
  industry leadership, 25
Calma, 109, 110, 112
Campbell, Robert, 38
Capacitators, ceramic, 1
Carterphone, 143
Casio, 25
Caterpillar Tractor, 116
Cathode ray tube, 73
CB radio, 18
Central Processing Unit (CPU), 12, 13
Cestari, Vincent M., 78
Chia Tung University, 74
Circuits, large-scale integrated, 21
Clevite, 25

Index

Cobol, 22
Commodore, 25
Commodore International, Ltd., 2, 31
Companies
  annual reports of, 44
  CAD/CAM, 105, 106, 109
  characteristics, 45, 46
  computer services, 77, 89, 90, 95, 96
  energy, 1
  hazards of buying into young, 48, 49
  health care, 1
  high-technology, 7, 8
  key designers in, 126
  machine tool, 113, 114, 115
  minicomputer, 69, 73
  software, 86, 88, 95, 100, 102, 103, 104
  solar cell, 1
  telecommunications, 1
  "10-K" report, 44
Computer-aided design. *See* CAD/CAM
Computer-aided manufacture. *See* CAD/CAM
Computer breakdown, 133, 134, 135, 136
Computer Consoles, 180
Computer memory, 51, 53
Computer-on-a-chip. *See* Microprocessor
Computer programing, 87
Computers
  core-memory 74
  knowledge of, 6
  mainframe, 2, 6, 15, 69, 72
  mainframe companies, 25
  micromainframe, 2
  mini, 69, 70, 71, 72
  in non-technical companies, 23, 24
  on-line systems, 135
  peripherals, 127
  prime past function of, 16
  research and development, 1
  specialized, 1
  terminals, 6
Computer Terminal Corp., 81
Computervision, 109, 110–112, 180
  research and development, 111
Condec Corp., 116
Control Data Corporation, 25, 126, 138
  Cyber 203 and 205, 139
Convertible debentures, 37, 38
Core-memory system, 74
Cray, Seymour R., 138
Cray Research, 2, 3, 126, 132, 138, 139, 146, 160, 161
  advantages, 141, 142
  Cray 1 S, 139
  debt, 142
  markets, 139, 140

P/E ratio, 147
  power of computers, 141
Cross & Trecker, 114, 115, 116
Cullinane, 23, 86
Cullinane Database Systems, 98, 99, 100, 103
Curve pricing. *See* Pricing; Product price control
Customer relations, 77, 78, 80
Cyclotron Corporation, 180
Czochralski method, 122, 123

Data banks, 1
Data base management, 98, 99, 100
Data General, 69, 70, 71, 72, 79
Datapoint Corporation, 73, 81, 83, 84, 180
  ARC, 81, 82
Data processing, 57, 69, 75, 81, 85, 88
  central system, 134
Data processor, 1
Datapro Reports, 158
Datapro Services, 45
Data Terminal Systems, 155, 156
Debt, 78, 79, 116, 142, 145,
  effect of on profits, 36, 37
  use of, 59, 60, 75, 154
DeForest, Lee, 12
Department of Energy, 122, 125
Digital Communications, 184
Digital Equipment Corporation, 69, 71, 72, 73, 79, 83, 156, 189
  Amdahl 470-V6, 91
  PDP-8 minicomputer, 91
Digital watch, 18
Dividends, 40, 156
Dow Jones Index, 149
Dun and Bradstreet, 22

Earnings growth rate, 28
Eberstadt, 99
Eberstadt's Surveyor, 164
Electricity, 124, 125
Electronic devices
  cost of, 16
  future, 18, 19
  new age, 17
  new products, 18
Emerson Electric, 179
Energy, 1, 8, 20
  shrinking supplies, 12
  thermal, 125
  in vegetation, 19
Eniac, 15, 16
Environment, importance of, 62
Equipment
  computer-aided design, 106

Index

electronics patient monitors, 24
laser-based microsurgery, 24
office, 77
Equity
   ownership, 64, 65, 67
   return on, 75, 76, 152, 153, 154, 155, 156, 169
Equity Research Associates, 148
Ethanol, 19
Evans & Sutherland, 110, 181
"EXPAND" network operating system, 137
Experience curve pricing, 54, 55
Exxon Corporation, 75

Factory, automated, 106
Fad stock syndrome, 48
Fairchild Camera, 49, 51
Fairchild Semiconductors, 49
Farrell, Robert, 5, 6
Federal Aviation Administration, 181
Financing, future expenditures, 38, 39
Finsilver, Joan M., 114, 115
First-time buyers, importance of, 157
First World Computing Services Industry Congress, 89
Fisher, Kenneth, 155
Flightsafety International, 181
Floating Point System, 181, 182
Flow General, 182, 183
Ford, Henry, 121
Fortran, 22
Fortune 500 companies, 127, 133, 143, 144
Four-Phase, 83
Fred Alger Management, Inc., 114
Friden, 25
Friden calculator, 93
Fuel, 9
   fossil, 12
   self-sufficiency in, 19

Gallium arsenide, 122
Gasahol, 19
G. D. Searle, 182
Genentech, 49, 93
   classic startup, 47, 48
General Electric, 24, 110, 163
General Motors, 97
Gerber Systems Technology, 109, 110
Giddings & Lewis, 116
Gistaro, E., 83
Greenfield, Samuel C., 159
Growth, rate of, 28, 169, 170, 171, 172
Growth company, prime requisites of, 35

Hambrecht and Quist, 29, 145
Harris Corporation, 83, 189

Harris Intertype Company, 113, 114
Hartwell, John, 142
Harvard Business Review, 50
Hewlett-Packard, 25, 74, 82, 126, 133, 154
Hoff, M. E., Jr., 12, 13, 51
Hoffman Electronics, 25
Honda of Japan, 119
Honeywell, Inc., 25, 75, 83
Hooker, John Jay, 170
Hyde, Clyde, 102

IBM, 2, 4, 5, 7, 13, 25, 71, 73, 74, 75, 78, 79, 82, 83, 99, 100, 102, 163, 189
   CAD/CAM candidate, 109
   compared with Cray, 141
   growth prospects, 171, 172
   IBM 1401, 94
   investment in, 3, 154
   Justice Department and, 173
   mainframe computer, 69
   management, 133
   multipurpose computers, 111
   new directions, 172
Ideology, 60
Industrial Revolution, 9, 16, 17
Inflation, 156
Ingersoll Milling Company, 116
"Inside information," 38, 39
Integraph, 109, 110
Intel Corporation, 2, 12, 13, 25, 39, 46, 70, 121, 129, 160, 161
   classic startup, 47
   competition, 49
   inventories, 58
   management, 49, 50, 56, 57
   micromainframe computer-on-three-silicon-chips, 58, 88
   m.o.s. technology, 54
   offices, 51
   semiconductor memory market, 59
   64 K RAMS, 60
   stock, 51, 52
   use of debt, 60
"Intellect," 22, 23
Investment strategy
   analysis, 160
   book value, 132, 152, 155, 156, 169
   company silhouette, 177
   conclusion, 190
   Datapro Reports, 158
   dividends, 40, 156
   earnings, 28, 140, 146, 169
   effect of greed, 168
   growth rate, 28, 169, 170
   importance of first-time buyers, 157

importance of management, 49, 50, 56, 57, 81, 84, 127, 133, 153
importance of repeat business, 157
institutional, 131
long-term, 129
low-high theory, 159, 160, 161
market maturity, 165, 166
market patterns, 129, 152, 159, 173, 174, 175
market potential, 5
market saturation, 166, 167
mutual funds, 40, 41, 42, 163
P/E ratio, 131, 132, 137, 138, 144, 145, 146, 147, 148, 149, 152
prices, 129, 131, 169
purchasing, 129, 131, 132, 158, 159, 162, 164
return on equity, 75, 76, 152, 153, 154, 155, 156, 169
selling, 157, 173, 174, 175
slow growth premiums, 168
suggested portfolio, 164
temporary setbacks, 129, 131
total market capitalization v. revenues, 147

John Fluke, 183
Jones, Peter Appleton, 141

Kaplan, Ralph, 35, 36
Kearney & Trecker, 114
Kevex Corporation, 183, 184
Kilby, Jack S., 119, 121, 127
KLA Instruments, 184
Kurlak, Tom P., 107, 108, 111

Labor unions, 115, 116
Ladenburg Thalman & Co., Inc., 148
Lamb, Joseph, 116
Language, 18, 22
Lautenberg, Frank R., 90, 91, 92, 93, 94, 95, 96
Lease business, 142
Linkabit, 184
Lockheed, 109

Macaleer, R. James, 100, 101, 102
Machines
  hospital, 24
  newspaper, 1, 2, 3, 24
M/A-Com, Inc., 184
Magid, Jim, 183
Mainframe computers, 2, 6, 15, 69, 72
Management
  data base, 98, 99, 100
  importance of, 49, 50, 56, 57, 81, 84, 127, 153
Marchant, 25

Market maturity, 165, 166
Market potential, 5
Market saturation, 166, 167
Masi, J. Carl, 77
Mathematica, 99
McClellan, Stephen T., 82, 83, 84
McGraw-Hill, 35
MCI Communications, 185
Medicaid, 101
Medical Technology Fund, Inc., 163, 164
Medicare, 101
Memory
  computer bank, 106
  devices, 55
Merrill Lynch, Pierce, Fenner & Smith, Inc., 5, 107, 111, 112
Microcomputer, 56
Microprocessors, 1, 9, 47, 51
  development of, 12, 13, 70
  future of, 14
  importance of, 13, 14
  thumb-nail sized, 2
  use of, 57
Microwave oven, 18
Minicomputers, 69–72
Minnie Pearl Chicken, 170, 171
Mitchell, Donald W., 144
Mitchell and Company, 152, 156
Mohawk, 83
Monroe, 25
Montgomery Securities, 139
Moody's *Investors' Service*, 44
Moore, Gordon E., 49, 50, 52–57
Morgan Stanley, 102, 138, 141
m.o.s. technology, 54
Motion pictures, 90
Motorola, 25, 125
Mutual funds, 40, 41, 42, 163

National Academy of Sciences, 7
National Semiconductor, 25
Nehra, John M., 102
Networking, 172
Newspaper companies, 23, 24
New York Times, The, 7, 18, 23, 43
Nippon Electronics, 185
Nixdorf, 83
Noyce, Robert N., 49, 50, 53, 121

Office automation, 76, 77, 78, 80, 82
Ohio-Scientific, 184
O'Kelley, Harold E., 81, 83
On-line computer systems, 135
OPEC, 34
Oppenheimer & Co. Inc., 99, 163
Oppenheimer Special Fund, 163, 164

Index

Palermo, Richard V., 83
Paradyne, 185
Payroll processing, 91, 92, 93
Pension funds, 5
Performance Systems, 171
Pertec, 83
Peter Principle, 56, 57
Photovoltaics, 20, 122, 123, 126
Polaroid, 4, 174
Poor, Victor D., 81, 83
Power
 low cost, 17
 solar, 19
Price, T. Rowe, 27–29
Price/earnings ratio, 131, 132, 137, 138, 144, 145, 146, 147, 148, 149, 152
Pricing, 54, 55, 58, 120, 121, 126
Prime Computer, 31, 153
 investment in, 154
Printer, fiber optics image, 79
Processing, distributed data v. mainframe computer, 82, 83
Processors, 1
Prodlin, 184
Product price control, 54, 55, 58
Programers, computer, 87, 88

Quarter-Million-Dollar Bonanza Club, 31–34

Radio, 17, 18, 90
Raytheon, 25, 83
RCA, 3, 24, 83, 163
Reliability factors, 15
Repeat business, importance of, 157
Research and development, 1, 111, 115, 121, 128
Robotics, 116
Rolm Corporation, 2, 31, 132
 debt, 145
 equipment, 143, 144
 marketing, 142, 143
 P/E ratio, 147
Rosen, Benjamin J., 16, 21, 24, 25, 121, 122, 123
Rowe Price New Horizons Fund, 148, 149
Rowe Price 2:1 Ratio rule, 148, 149, 152
"Rule of 72," 28

Salomon Brothers, 82
Sanders, W. Jerry, III, 21, 60–67, 189
Sanders Associates, 109
Schlumberger, 51, 110
Scientific-Atlanta, 186
Scientists, management of, 50, 51
Scitex America Corporation, 186
Second Industrial Revolution, 7, 11

Securities and Exchange Commission, 44
Security analysts, 113, 141, 172
 Berdell, 139
 Finsilver, 114, 115
 Kurlak, 107, 108, 111
 McClellan, 82, 83, 84
 Rosen, 16, 21, 24, 25, 121–124
 Weils, 138, 141
Security Services, Inc., 38
Semiconductors, 20, 21, 24, 25, 39, 54
 industry leadership, 25
 memory market, 59
 metal oxide technology, 62
Shared Medical Systems, 100–103, 133
Sharp, 25
Sherve, Dennis Q., 102
Shockley Semiconductor Laboratory, 49
Silicon, 12, 54, 123, 124
 Czochralski method, 122, 123
 photovoltaics, 20, 122, 123, 126
Silicon chips, 53
Silicon Valley, 51, 59, 64
Smith Barney Harris Upham, 127
Software, 70, 76, 78, 81, 86, 87, 88, 89, 95, 100, 102, 103, 104, 108, 143
Solar cells, 1, 122
Solar power, 19, 118, 123
 economics of, 125
 markets, 118
 rooftop energy devices, 119
Solar systems, 20, 125
Sony Corporation, 146
Spectra Physics, 186, 187
Sperry Rand Corporation, 3, 15, 16, 163
Standard of living, 12
Standard & Poor's, 29
 500 stocks, 147, 148, 149
 Stock Guide, 44
 Stock Reports, 176
Start-ups, 47–49, 52, 53
Stasen, George J., 163
Stock market
 high technology and, 1, 5, 6
 professionals, 7
Stocks, 7, 8, 22, 25
 computer-based, 24
 earlier era growth, 4
 selection for rewards, 3, 4
Storage Technology, 127
Sycor, 83
Sylvania, 24

Tandem Computer, 126, 132–137, 146, 160, 161, 187
 debt, 138
 P/E ratio, 147

Index

Tandy's Radio Shack, 25, 146
Tapes, numerical control, 106
Taub, Henry, 91, 92
Technology, high, 1
  bipolar, 62
  ideology in, 60
  importance of environment, 62
  metal oxide semiconductor, 62
  semiconductor, 20, 21
Telecommunications, 1
Television, 18, 90
"10-K" report, 44
Texas Instruments, 25, 54, 70, 124, 125, 127, 160, 161
  management, 127
  pricing policy, 120, 121
  research and development, 121, 128
  solar panels, 125, 126
  solar power, 119, 120, 122
  TI-Kilby method, 122, 123
Thermostats, 18
Three Faces of Eve, 96
TI-Kilby method, 122, 123
Topol, Sidney, 186
Total market capitalization *v.* revenues, 147
Transistor, 12, 13

Unimation, 116, 117, 188
United States Surgical Corporation, 187
Univac, 15, 25, 83

University Patents, 187, 188
U.S. Post Office, 76

Vacuum tube industry, 24, 25
Value Line Investment Survey, 44, 75, 79, 116, 153, 176
Victor, 25
Victor Comptometers, 93
Video cassette recorder, 18
Vydec terminal, 75

Wang, Dr. An, 73–75, 79
Wang Computer, 2
Wang Laboratories, 31, 72, 73, 80, 82, 84, 160, 161, 188
  debt, 78, 79
Wang's Mailway, 76
Warner Lambert, 146
Washington Post, 23
Weather forecasts, 2, 140, 141
Weil, Frederica, 138, 141
Weil, Ulric, 138, 141
Westergaard, John, 148, 149, 152, 184, 186, 187
Western Electric, 66
Westinghouse, 25
Wilson, Harvey J., 102
Wireless telegraphy, 17
Word processing systems, 73, 74, 75, 113
Word processors, 1, 73, 74

Xerox Corporation, 7, 75